DIPS, SPREADS, NOSH

OVER 100 RECIPES FOR EASY AND ELEGANT ENTERTAINING

13-Digit ISBN: 978-1-60433-885-0
10-Digit ISBN: 1-60433-885-7

This book may be ordered by mail from the publisher. Please include $5.99 for postage and handling. Please support your local bookseller first!

Books published by Cider Mill Press Book Publishers are available at special discounts for bulk purchases in the United States by corporations, institutions, and other organizations. For more information, please contact the publisher.

Cider Mill Press Book Publishers
"Where good books are ready for press"
PO Box 454
12 Spring Street
Kennebunkport, Maine 04046
Visit us online!
cidermillpress.com

Typography: Bushcraft, Adobe Garamond, Clarendon, Fenway Park, Sentinel Black, Helvetica Round, and Neutraface 2
Image Credits: Images on pages 26, 50, 56, 59, 69, 70, 72, 75, 76, 96, 102, 178, 182, 213, 214, 223, 226 courtesy of Cider Mill Press. All other images used under official license from Shutterstock.com.

Printed in the USA
2 3 4 5 6 7 8 9 0

DIPS, SPREADS, NOSH

OVER 100 RECIPES FOR EASY AND ELEGANT ENTERTAINING

CIDER MILL PRESS

BOOK PUBLISHERS
KENNEBUNKPORT, MAINE

Contents

Introduction

When the serving board comes out, it means something special is about to happen. It seems impossible, but that humble wooden board can easily become the most extravagant serving piece at a table. Its ability to mirror the mood of a host and transform a room's ambiance renders a standard plate boring and ineffectual.

Whether it is a gorgeous assortment of hard-to-obtain cheeses for a formal dinner party, or a simple afternoon nibble of nuts and sliced fruit to go with a chilled glass of rosé, serving anything on a board instantly elevates the moment. Large or small, round or rectangular, unfinished or polished, a board can take many forms. But no matter what, it is always a welcome sight.

Traditionally, it is used to showcase something beautiful: a few perfect tomatoes from the garden, a wedge of cheese recommended by a local cheese monger, or a luxurious pile of cured meat. Whether it is presenting these, a loaf of bread fresh from the oven, olives a friend brought back from their travels, or a beautiful handmade preserve and a handful of crackers you baked yourself, the serving board is a blank canvas, made to let you craft, slice, and display limitless combinations of foodstuffs that suit your tastes and moods.

From experts to amateurs, everyone is in full agreement that the board itself is the foundation of greatness, no matter what form it may take. It always has a couple of great stories to tell: the contents sum up the party, and its scarred surface relates the snacks and meals gone by. Most importantly, a beautiful board always leads to conversation, which is what we're all after, in the end.

Crackers and Breads

One of the many appealing aspects of centering parties and meals around serving boards is that many little bites can be had. Perhaps you fill up a plate with whatever's on offer, or perhaps you pick and choose as the noshing spirit strikes, a cube of cheese here, a slice of meat there. But as you will see, serving boards are about much more than meat and cheese, and the recipes that follow provide a wide range of textures and flavor profiles that will enhance whatever you decide to populate your board with.

Sea Salt and Herb Crackers

YIELD: 12 CRACKERS • ACTIVE TIME: 10 MINUTES
TOTAL TIME: 1 HOUR AND 15 MINUTES

These light crackers will add just enough flavor to enhance whatever you choose to top them with.

1 Preheat oven to 425°F.

2 Mix the flour, baking powder, water, olive oil, fine sea salt, paprika, and pepper in a small bowl. Let rest in the refrigerator for an hour.

3 Line a baking sheet with parchment.

4 Form the dough into small balls and roll them out into long, paper-thin rectangles.

5 Place the crackers on a baking sheet and brush generously with olive oil. Sprinkle with flaky sea salt and fresh herbs.

6 Bake for 5 minutes, or until the crackers are golden brown. Let cool on a wire rack before serving.

INGREDIENTS

2 cups all-purpose flour, plus more for dusting

1½ teaspoons baking powder

1 cup water

3 tablespoons olive oil, plus more for brushing

1 teaspoon fine sea salt

1 teaspoon paprika

1 teaspoon black pepper

Flaky sea salt, to taste

Fresh herbs, finely chopped

Rosemary Crackers

YIELD: 6 CRACKERS • ACTIVE TIME: 15 MINUTES • TOTAL TIME: 1 HOUR

If you're thinking of loading up your board with meat, you should take advantage of the sharp flavor provided by these crackers.

INGREDIENTS

⅛ teaspoon dried yeast

1 tablespoon warm water (110 to 115°F)

¾ cup all-purpose flour, plus more for dusting

½ teaspoon salt

Pinch of sugar

1 tablespoon fresh rosemary, leaves removed and chopped

Olive oil, for brushing

1 Preheat oven to 350°F.

2 Place the yeast and the warm water in a bowl and let stand for 10 minutes.

3 Add the remaining ingredients to the bowl and knead until a smooth dough forms.

4 Cover and let stand in a warm spot for 15 to 20 minutes, or until the dough doubles in size.

5 On a lightly floured surface, roll out the dough as thin as you can without tearing it.

6 Cut crackers to desired shape and place on a parchment-lined baking sheet. Brush the crackers with a small amount of olive oil.

7 Place in oven and bake for 20 minutes, or until golden brown. Let cool on a wire rack before serving.

Purple Potato Chips

YIELD: 4 TO 6 SERVINGS • ACTIVE TIME: 5 MINUTES • TOTAL TIME: 20 MINUTES

Purple potato chips add a completely unique presentation aspect to your board and go well with any dip.

1 Preheat oven to 400°F.

2 Thinly slice the potatoes. Use a mandoline for extremely thin chips, or to create ruffled edges.

3 Place the potatoes and the olive oil in a bowl and toss until the potatoes are evenly coated. Place the potatoes on a baking sheet in a single layer. Bake for 12 to 15 minutes, or until crispy.

4 Remove from the oven, transfer to a bowl, add the salt, and toss lightly. Serve warm or store in an airtight container.

INGREDIENTS

3 large purple potatoes

4 tablespoons olive oil

2 teaspoons sea salt

Beet Chips

YIELD: 4 TO 6 SERVINGS • ACTIVE TIME: 5 MINUTES • TOTAL TIME: 20 MINUTES

These bloodred roots make beautiful and delicious crispy snacks.

INGREDIENTS

5 fresh beets, peeled

4 tablespoons olive oil

2 teaspoons sea salt

1 Preheat the oven to 400°F.

2 Thinly slice the beets. Place the beets and the olive oil in a bowl and toss until the slices are evenly coated. Place on a baking sheet in a single layer. Bake for 12 to 15 minutes, or until golden brown.

3 Remove from the oven, transfer to a bowl, add the salt, and toss. Serve warm or store in an airtight container.

Rye Crackers

The earthy, spicy flavor of rye makes these crackers a welcome addition to any board.

1 Preheat the oven to 350°F.

2 Mix all ingredients other than the seeds in a bowl. Place the dough on a flour-dusted surface and roll it out until approximately ¼-inch thick. Use cookie cutters to shape the crackers and, if desired, sprinkle with sesame and/or sunflower seeds. If desired, use a fork to punch some small holes in the crackers.

3 Place the crackers on a parchment-lined baking sheet and bake for 20 minutes. Let cool on a wire rack before serving.

INGREDIENTS

2 cups rye flour, plus more for dusting

2 teaspoons salt

Freshly ground black pepper, to taste

1 cup olive oil

2 cups water

2 tablespoons sesame and/or sunflower seeds (optional)

Parmesan Crisps

YIELD: 8 CRISPS • ACTIVE TIME: 5 MINUTES • TOTAL TIME: 10 MINUTES

These simple, lacy crisps are quick and can be made well in advance. They are best stored in an airtight container.

INGREDIENTS

½ cup Parmesan cheese, grated

1 Preheat oven to 400°F.

2 Pour a tablespoon of Parmesan onto a parchment-lined baking sheet and lightly pat down. Repeat with the remaining cheese, spacing each spoonful about ½-inch apart.

3 Bake for 3 to 5 minutes, or until golden and crisp. Let cool on a wire rack before serving.

Crispy Wonton Skins

YIELD: 4 TO 6 SERVINGS • ACTIVE TIME: 5 MINUTES • TOTAL TIME: 10 MINUTES

Made from simple wonton wrappers, these crispy "skins" go especially well with Asian-inspired dips.

INGREDIENTS

2 cups vegetable oil

4 wonton wrappers, cut into triangles

Salt, to taste

1 Place the oil in a Dutch oven and cook over medium-high heat until it is 300°F.

2 Place the wonton wrappers in the Dutch oven and turn frequently until crispy and golden brown.

3 Use a slotted spoon to remove the fried wonton wrappers from the oil and set on paper towels to drain.

4 Season with salt and serve.

Prosciutto Chips

YIELD: 4 TO 6 SERVINGS • ACTIVE TIME: 3 MINUTES
TOTAL TIME: 15 TO 18 MINUTES

Charcuterie and chips combined, these are an elegant addition to any spread.

INGREDIENTS

20 slices of prosciutto, sliced thin

1 Preheat oven to 400°F. Lay slices of prosciutto flat on a baking sheet. Don't worry about placing the slices too close together as they will shrink as they cook.

2 Place baking sheet in the oven and bake for 12 to 15 minutes, or until the prosciutto is crispy. Serve warm.

Caraway Water Biscuits

Biscuits that are light and airy enough to elevate any occasion.

1 Preheat oven to 350°F.

2 Add the flour and water to a mixing bowl and whisk until combined. Add the salt.

3 On a parchment-lined baking sheet, use a pastry brush to transfer the batter to the sheet, taking care to make nice, long crackers.

4 Sprinkle with caraway seeds and place in the oven. Bake for 8 minutes, or until golden brown. Remove the sheet and let the crackers cool before serving.

INGREDIENTS

⅛ cup all-purpose flour

10 tablespoons water

⅛ teaspoon salt

2 tablespoons caraway seeds

Cheese Twists

YIELD: 12 TO 15 SERVINGS • ACTIVE TIME: 15 TO 20 MINUTES
TOTAL TIME: 30 MINUTES

Feel free to try other combinations of cheeses to create different-tasting twists.

INGREDIENTS

2 puff pastry sheets, thawed

½ cup Fontina cheese, grated

½ cup Parmesan cheese, grated

1 teaspoon fresh thyme, minced

1 teaspoon freshly ground black pepper

1 egg, beaten

1 Preheat oven to 375°F.

2 Roll out puff pastry until the sheets are approximately 10 by 12 inches.

3 In a bowl, combine the cheeses, thyme, and pepper.

4 Lightly brush the tops of the pastry sheets with the egg. Then, sprinkle the cheese mixture over the pastry sheets and lightly press down so the mixture sticks to the surface.

5 Cut the sheets into ¼-inch thick strips and twist. Then, place twists on a baking sheet. Bake for 12 to 15 minutes, or until twists are golden brown and puffy. Turn over each twist to ensure even browning and allow to cook for an additional 2 to 3 minutes.

6 Remove twists from the oven and let cool on a wire rack before serving.

Pretzels

**YIELD: 8 PRETZELS • ACTIVE TIME: 20 MINUTES
TOTAL TIME: 1 HOUR AND 20 MINUTES**

Pair these pretzels with your favorite ale and horseradish or mustard.

1 Preheat oven to 450°F.

2 Combine the yeast, 110°F water, and sugar in a small bowl and let sit for 10 minutes until frothy. Add the flour and salt. Mix by hand for a few seconds to roughly combine, then knead. The dough should feel soft and smooth.

3 Cover and let rise for 30 minutes.

4 Grease a baking sheet with vegetable oil.

5 Place the dough onto a lightly oiled countertop and cut it into eight pieces.

6 Combine the warm water and baking soda and microwave for 1 minute.

7 Roll each of the eight pieces into a long rope, then shape into pretzels. Dip each pretzel into the baking soda-and-water mixture then transfer to the greased baking sheet. Sprinkle with the coarse sea salt and let rest for 10 minutes.

8 Bake for 9 to 10 minutes until the pretzels are golden brown. Once out of the oven, brush the pretzels with the melted butter while they are still hot.

INGREDIENTS

2¼ teaspoons instant yeast

1 cup water

Olive oil, for baking sheet

1 teaspoon sugar

2½ cups all-purpose flour

½ teaspoon sea salt

Vegetable oil, for greasing baking sheet, plus more for countertop

½ cup warm water

1 tablespoon baking soda

Coarse sea salt, for topping

3 tablespoons unsalted butter, melted

Cornbread with Honey

YIELD: 16 SERVINGS • ACTIVE TIME: 40 MINUTES
TOTAL TIME: 2 HOURS AND 15 MINUTES

This savory bread pairs well with fresh vegetables and sweet spreads.

INGREDIENTS

5 ears of corn

10 tablespoons unsalted butter, cut into tablespoons

1 cup diced onion

1 tablespoon minced garlic

2½ tablespoons salt, plus more to taste

2¾ cups heavy cream

2 cups all-purpose flour

2 cups cornmeal

¼ cup brown sugar

2 tablespoons baking powder

½ teaspoon cayenne pepper

½ teaspoon paprika

1½ cups honey

6 eggs

¼ cup sour cream

1 Preheat the oven to 400°F.

2 Place the ears of corn on a baking sheet, place it in the oven, and bake for 25 minutes, until the kernels have a slight give to them. Remove from the oven and let cool. When the ears of corn are cool enough to handle, remove the husks and silk and cut the kernels from the cob. Reserve the corn cobs for another preparation. Lower the oven temperature to 300°F.

3 Place 2 tablespoons of the butter in a large saucepan and melt over medium heat. Add the onion and garlic, season with salt, and cook until the onion is translucent.

Set ¾ cup of the corn kernels aside and add the rest to the pan. Add 2 cups of the cream and cook until the corn is very tender, about 15 to 20 minutes.

4 Strain, reserve the cream, and transfer the solids to the blender. Puree until smooth, adding the cream as needed if the mixture is too thick. Season to taste and allow the puree to cool completely.

5 Place the flour, cornmeal, 2½ tablespoons of salt, brown sugar, baking powder, cayenne pepper, and paprika in a large mixing bowl and stir until combined. Place 2 cups of the corn puree, the honey, eggs, remaining cream, and sour cream in a separate large mixing bowl and stir until combined. Gradually add the dry mixture to the wet mixture and whisk to combine. When all of the dry mixture has been incorporated, add the reserved corn kernels and fold the mixture until they are evenly distributed.

6 Grease an 11 x 7-inch baking pan and pour the batter into it. Place the pan in the oven and bake until a toothpick inserted into the center comes out clean, about 35 minutes. Remove from the oven and briefly cool before cutting.

Dense Fruit Bread

YIELD: 1 LOAF • ACTIVE TIME: 15 MINUTES • TOTAL TIME: 1½ HOURS

Tweaking a recipe from the well-known blog *Not Quite Nigella* resulted in this decadent bread.

1 Preheat oven to 350°F and line a standard loaf pan with parchment paper.

2 Place fruit and 2 cups of apple cider in a saucepan and bring to a simmer. Allow to simmer for 20 minutes or until the fruit has absorbed the liquid. Stir in baking soda and set aside.

3 Add the brown sugar, flour, cinnamon, and ginger to a small bowl and stir until well combined. Stir in the eggs. Then, add the fruit mixture and the remaining apple cider. Stir until well combined and pour into prepared loaf pan.

4 Bake for 45 minutes or until an inserted skewer comes out clean. Remove from the oven and let cool for a few minutes. Run a knife around the pan to loosen, then unmold and transfer to a wire rack to cool. Top with sea salt and melted butter before slicing.

INGREDIENTS

¾ cup prunes

1¼ cup dried cranberries

¾ cup pitted dates

1 cup golden raisins

3 cups apple cider

1 teaspoon baking soda

½ cup brown sugar

2 cups all-purpose flour

2 teaspoons ground cinnamon

1 teaspoon ground ginger

2 eggs

Coarse sea salt, for topping

3 tablespoons unsalted butter, melted

New England Brown Bread

YIELD: 1 LOAF • ACTIVE TIME: 15 MINUTES • TOTAL TIME: 1 HOUR

This sweet bread can be served with anything pungent or salty. Slices of grilled sausages and spicy mustard are also good partners.

INGREDIENTS

Butter, for greasing coffee can or loaf pan

½ cup all-purpose flour

½ cup rye flour

½ cup finely ground cornmeal

½ teaspoon baking powder

½ teaspoon baking soda

½ teaspoon salt

½ teaspoon nutmeg

1 cup buttermilk

½ cup molasses

1 Preheat oven to 325°F.

2 Bring a pot of water to a boil.

3 Grease a standard coffee can or a small loaf pan with the butter.

4 In a large bowl, mix together the flours, cornmeal, baking powder, baking soda, salt, and nutmeg.

5 In another bowl, whisk together the buttermilk and molasses.

6 Combine the wet and dry ingredients and stir well with a spoon. Pour batter into can or pan, making sure to only fill about two-thirds of the way.

7 Cover the loaf pan or coffee can tightly with foil and place it into a baking pan.

8 Pour the boiling water into the baking pan until it reaches one-third of the way up the side of the coffee can or loaf pan. Put the baking pan into the oven.

9 Bake for 45 minutes or until a toothpick inserted into the middle comes out clean. Let cool slightly before serving.

Classic Stout Bread

YIELD: 2 LOAVES • ACTIVE TIME: 10 MINUTES
TOTAL TIME: 1 HOUR AND 10 MINUTES

This recipe is best served with slices of sharp cheddar.

1 Preheat oven to 400°F and grease 2 loaf pans.

2 Stir dry ingredients in a bowl and set aside. In a separate bowl, combine the butter, buttermilk, and beer.

3 Place the wet and dry ingredients together and stir until well combined. Pour into prepared loaf pans and sprinkle with additional oats.

4 Bake for 1 hour or until a knife inserted into the middle of the loaves comes out clean. Let cool on a wire rack before serving.

INGREDIENTS

2¼ cups whole wheat flour

1 cup rolled oats, plus more for topping

½ cup brown sugar

2¼ teaspoons baking soda

1 teaspoon baking powder

½ teaspoon salt

⅓ cup butter, melted

1 cup buttermilk

1 bottle of Guinness or other stout

Classic Pita Bread

YIELD: 16 PITAS • ACTIVE TIME: 30 MINUTES • TOTAL TIME: 2½ HOURS

Here's an easy recipe for a flatbread that originated in the Mediterranean region, purportedly ancient Greece. It is popular around the world.

INGREDIENTS

1 packet (2¼ teaspoons) active dry yeast

2½ cups water (110 to 115°F)

3 cups flour

1 tablespoon olive oil, plus more for skillet

1 tablespoon salt

3 cups whole wheat flour

Butter, for coating the bowl

1 Proof the yeast by mixing with the warm water. Let sit for about 10 minutes until foamy.

2 In a large bowl, add the yeast mix into the regular flour and stir until it forms a stiff dough. Cover and let the dough rise for about 1 hour.

3 Add the oil and salt to the dough and stir in the whole wheat flour in half-cup increments. When finished, the dough should be soft. Turn onto a lightly floured surface and knead it until it is smooth and elastic, about 10 minutes.

4 Coat the bottom and sides of a large mixing bowl (ceramic is best) with butter. Place the ball of dough in the bowl, cover loosely with plastic wrap, put it in a naturally warm, draft-free location, and let it rise until doubled in size, about 45 minutes to 1 hour.

5 On a lightly floured surface, punch down the dough and cut into 16 pieces. Put the pieces on a baking sheet and cover with a dish towel while working with individual pieces.

6 Roll out the pieces with a rolling pin until they are approximately 7 inches across. Stack them between sheets of plastic wrap.

7 Heat the skillet over high heat and lightly oil the bottom. Cook the individual pitas about 20 seconds on one side, then flip and cook for about a minute on the other side, until bubbles form. Turn again and continue to cook until the pita puffs up, another minute or so. Keep the skillet lightly oiled while processing, and store the pitas on a plate under a clean dish towel until ready to serve.

Quick Baguette

Adapted from Mark Bittman, this simple baguette can be the star on any board, especially when people find out you made it yourself.

INGREDIENTS

2¼ teaspoons active dry yeast

1 cup water (110 to 115°F)

3½ cups all-purpose flour, plus more for dusting

2 teaspoons salt

1 Preheat oven to 400°F.

2 In a large bowl, mix yeast into the water and let sit 5 minutes. Add 3 cups of the flour and the salt. Mix until combined.

3 Knead until dough is smooth and elastic. Shape dough into a ball and place in a lightly greased bowl. Cover with plastic wrap and let rise until doubled in size, about 1 hour.

4 Punch down the dough and divide it into two pieces. Roll each piece into a foot-long loaf.

5 Place the loaves side by side, about 3 to 4 inches apart, on a baking sheet lined with floured parchment paper.

6 Cover with plastic wrap. Let the loaves rise for about 30 minutes and remove plastic wrap. Using a sharp knife, score the top of each loaf, making diagonal slits that are approximately ½-inch deep.

7 Place baguettes in oven. Reduce heat to 375°F and bake until golden brown, about 20 to 25 minutes. The inside of the bread should read close to 210°F on a thermometer when it is done.

8 Remove from the oven and spritz with water.

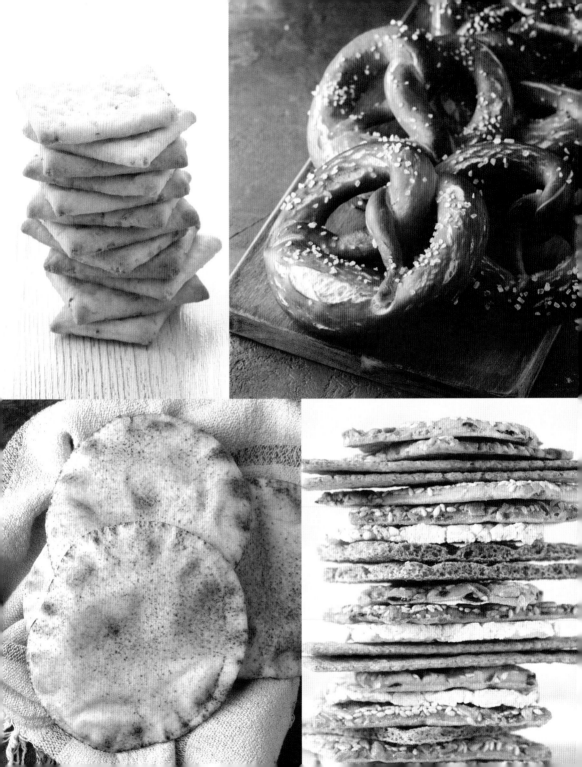

Cheese

While the dizzying styles and varieties of cheese can be intimidating, there is no shortage of fine cheesemakers and world-class cheese mongers whose expertise will help you identify which selections and preparations are right for your serving board.

Baked Cheese

A soft cheese warmed up so it becomes gooey goodness is enhanced by the addition of sweet, fruity accompaniments or savory, filling toppings.

INGREDIENTS

8 oz. Brie or Camembert cheese

1 baguette, sliced

For Savory Topping:

¼ cup roasted tomatoes, chopped

¼ cup jarred artichokes, chopped

2 tablespoons pitted olives, chopped

1 tablespoon capers

Pinch of black pepper

For Sweet Topping:

¼ cup pecans, chopped

¼ cup dried apricots, chopped

⅓ cup fig spread

¼ cup dried cherries

Pinch of ground cinnamon

1 Preheat oven to 350°F.

2 Place your cheese in a ceramic Brie baker and top it with your topping of choice.

3 Bake for 15 minutes, or until cheese is gooey.

4 Remove from oven. Serve with slices of baguette, which are intended to be dipped directly into the cheese.

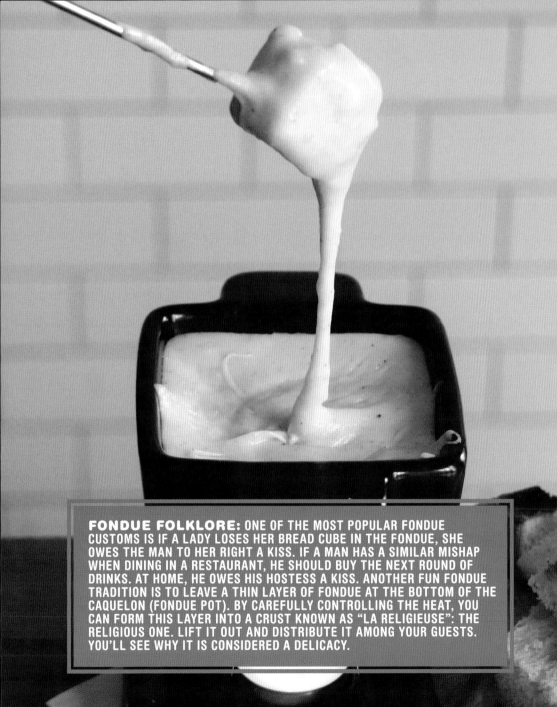

FONDUE FOLKLORE: ONE OF THE MOST POPULAR FONDUE CUSTOMS IS IF A LADY LOSES HER BREAD CUBE IN THE FONDUE, SHE OWES THE MAN TO HER RIGHT A KISS. IF A MAN HAS A SIMILAR MISHAP WHEN DINING IN A RESTAURANT, HE SHOULD BUY THE NEXT ROUND OF DRINKS. AT HOME, HE OWES HIS HOSTESS A KISS. ANOTHER FUN FONDUE TRADITION IS TO LEAVE A THIN LAYER OF FONDUE AT THE BOTTOM OF THE CAQUELON (FONDUE POT). BY CAREFULLY CONTROLLING THE HEAT, YOU CAN FORM THIS LAYER INTO A CRUST KNOWN AS "LA RELIGIEUSE": THE RELIGIOUS ONE. LIFT IT OUT AND DISTRIBUTE IT AMONG YOUR GUESTS. YOU'LL SEE WHY IT IS CONSIDERED A DELICACY.

Classic Fondue

Some recommendations to serve along with this delicious fondue are: cornichons, Genoa salami, Calabrese salami, crusty bread, cipollini onions, boiled potatoes, and soppressata.

1 In a bowl, toss the cheeses with the cornstarch until the cheese is well-coated.

2 Cut the garlic clove in half. Rub the inside of a crock-pot or fondue pot with garlic, then add the wine and lemon juice and bring to a simmer over low heat.

3 Add the cheese mixture all at once. Using a wooden spoon, stir over medium-low heat until the cheese is melted and smooth, about 5 to 10 minutes.

4 Season with salt, pepper, and grated nutmeg.

5 Dip your favorite accompaniments into the fondue and enjoy with friends.

INGREDIENTS

1 lb. Gruyère cheese, grated

½ lb. Emmentaler cheese, grated

½ lb. Gouda cheese, grated

2 tablespoons cornstarch

1 garlic clove

1 cup white wine

1 tablespoon lemon juice

Salt, pepper, and grated nutmeg, to taste

Beer Cheese

Almost any bread or cracker will go well with this cheese, but pretzel rolls are what those in the know go with.

INGREDIENTS

1 lb. cheddar cheese, grated

4 oz. cream cheese, at room temperature

1 garlic clove, finely grated

¼ cup red wine

1 tablespoon whole grain mustard

1 teaspoon Dijon mustard

2 teaspoons Worcestershire sauce

½ teaspoon paprika

1 cup brown ale, at room temperature

Pretzel rolls, to serve (optional)

1 Put all of the ingredients in a food processor, except for the beer, and puree until well combined.

2 Pour in ½ cup of the beer and continue to blend. Slowly add the rest of the beer a bit at a time, blending between each addition.

3 Cover and refrigerate for 1 hour before serving.

4 If using, toast the pretzel rolls in the oven until warmed through.

Fromage Blanc with Herbs

YIELD: 4 TO 6 SERVINGS • ACTIVE TIME: 5 MINUTES • TOTAL TIME: 5 MINUTES

This French classic is traditionally served as a starter, but it works well as a dip or spread.

INGREDIENTS

4 oz. fromage blanc

Zest of 6 lemons

4 tablespoons lemon juice

3 tablespoons fresh parsley, minced

3 tablespoons fresh mint, minced

3 tablespoons fresh dill, minced

Salt and pepper, to taste

1 Combine all ingredients in the bowl of a 5-quart mixer. Mix with paddle attachment until well combined.

NOTE: QUARK IS A CREAMY, UNRIPE CHEESE THAT IS POPULAR IN GERMANY AND EASTERN EUROPEAN COUNTRIES. IF YOU'RE INTRIGUED, CHECK OUT YOUR LOCAL DAIRY FARM.

Summer Vegetable Cheese Dip

YIELD: 4 TO 6 SERVINGS • ACTIVE TIME: 20 MINUTES
TOTAL TIME: 1 HOUR AND 45 MINUTES

This versatile dip has the ability to accommodate leafy greens, slices of crusty bread, and almost any vegetable.

1 Place the cream cheese or quark, sour cream, and mozzarella in a bowl and stir until well combined.

2 Add the remaining ingredients for the dip, stir to combine, and place in the refrigerator for at least 1 hour.

3 Approximately 30 minutes before you are ready to serve the dip, preheat the oven to 350°F.

4 Transfer the dip to an oven-safe bowl, top with additional mozzarella, and bake until the cheese is melted and starting to brown, about 20 minutes. Remove from the oven and serve warm with slices of crusty bread.

INGREDIENTS

1 cup cream cheese or quark cheese

½ cup sour cream

1 cup mozzarella cheese, grated plus more for topping

2 tablespoons fresh rosemary leaves

2 tablespoons fresh thyme leaves

½ cup diced summer squash

1 cup Swiss chard

1 cup spinach

6 garlic cloves, diced

2 teaspoons salt

1 teaspoon pepper

Slices of crusty bread, to serve

Baked St. Albans

A spoonful of fruit jam adorns the top of rich and creamy cheese and a sheet of puff pastry covers its rind.

INGREDIENTS

1 package of soft cow's milk cheese like Brie or Saint-Marcellin

1 tablespoon raspberry jam

1 sheet of puff pastry, thawed

1 baguette, sliced

1 Preheat oven to 350°F.

2 Spoon the jam onto the top of the cheese.

3 Cut the sheet of puff pastry into a square slightly larger than the crock that the cheese comes in. Dampen the bottom edge of the sheet with water, then gently lay it over the cheese, pressing down to seal.

4 Place the crock on a baking sheet or in a baking dish. Bake for 20 minutes, or until pastry is lightly brown and crispy.

5 Serve immediately with the sliced baguette.

TIP: YOU CAN INCLUDE ROASTED GARLIC CLOVES OR A PINCH OF RED PEPPER FLAKES TO BOOST THE FLAVOR.

Herb-Marinated Goat Cheese

YIELD: 4 TO 6 SERVINGS • ACTIVE TIME: 10 MINUTES
TOTAL TIME: 1 HOUR 10 MINUTES

This herb-marinated goat cheese will travel well and is perfect for a picnic. A selection of fresh, seasonal herbs soaked in olive oil infuse the goat cheese with deliciously vibrant flavors, while still allowing the cheese's tanginess to shine through.

1 Remove fresh goat cheese logs from wrapper and slice into thick rounds.

2 Gently roll cheese rounds in the herbs and press so that the herbs adhere to the surface of the cheese.

3 Layer the goat cheese rounds in glass jars. Pour olive oil over the cheese until it's almost covered.

4 Let marinate for an hour before serving with grilled bread or crackers. Can be stored for up to a week in the fridge.

INGREDIENTS

8 oz. fresh goat cheese

⅓ cup fresh herbs, chopped (tarragon, chives, and thyme are recommended)

1 cup extra virgin olive oil

Grilled bread or crackers, to serve

Goat Cheese–Stuffed Peppadew Peppers

YIELD: 4 TO 6 SERVINGS • ACTIVE TIME: 5 MINUTES • TOTAL TIME: 5 MINUTES

These are an easy-to-prepare, no-frills fan favorite on a cheese board, or served amongst tapas at a summer gathering. The sweet and tart peppers pair perfectly with the creaminess of spreadable goat cheese. This dish stores well in the fridge, so it can be prepared ahead of time.

INGREDIENTS

4 oz. spreadable goat cheese

¾ cup Peppadew peppers

2 tablespoons extra virgin olive oil

4 tablespoons fresh basil, chopped

Grilled bread or crackers, to serve

1 Stir the spreadable goat cheese. Then, spoon into either a piping bag with a small round tip or a sandwich bag with a small hole cut into one corner.

2 Drain the Peppadew peppers, but don't rinse.

3 Using the piping or sandwich bag, fill each pepper with goat cheese and place them on a plate.

4 Once all the peppers are filled, drizzle olive oil on top and sprinkle with the basil. Serve with grilled bread or crackers.

Boards for All Seasons

Filled with arrays of hard and soft cheeses, in-season fruits, pungent cured meats, creamy dips, and punchy pickles, a thoughtfully arranged, bountiful serving board can appeal to and satisfy anyone. They become centerpieces of social gatherings, causing us to gather and talk as we enjoy what's on offer. Serving boards are informal but can be fancy; they can be a collection of snacks or a carefully composed meal.

They are whatever you want to make them. What follows are arrestingly beautiful boards created by Vermont Creamery that can either be emulated or used as the inspiration for your own medley.

Spring Board for Success

When the ground has thawed but there's still a chill in the air, you want to capture the excitement of renewal and ensure that no one leaves hungry. This lovely blend of light and hearty bites has you covered.

INGREDIENTS

Assorted goat cheeses

Assorted aged cheeses

Charcuterie (such as hard salami, prosciutto, and soppressata)

Fresh vegetables (such as snow peas, broccoli, and celery)

Pickled Asparagus (see page 139)

Herb-Roasted Almonds (see page 120)

Beer Cheese (see page 52)

Black Olive Tapenade (see page 156)

Pickled Beets (see page 140)

Cornbread with Honey (see page 32)

1 Take cheeses out of the fridge 1 hour prior to serving and allow to come to room temperature.

2 Arrange the ingredients on a serving board.

Summer Antipasto Cheeseboard

YIELD: 4 TO 6 SERVINGS • ACTIVE TIME: 5 MINUTES • TOTAL TIME: 1 HOUR

The last thing you want to do in the summer is stand around a hot kitchen. This board will get you out with your friends and family and keep you cool.

INGREDIENTS

Assorted fresh goat cheeses

Assorted aged cheeses

Goat Cheese–Stuffed Peppadew peppers (see page 62)

Herb-Marinated Goat Cheese (see page 61)

Charcuterie (such as hard salami, prosciutto, and speck)

Nuts, roasted (Marcona almonds and pecans work well)

Fresh vegetables (tomatoes and cucumbers are good options)

Grilled bread and pita wedges

Hummus

Pepperoncini

Assorted olives

Honey

1 Take cheeses out of the fridge 1 hour prior to serving and allow to come to room temperature.

2 Arrange the ingredients on a serving board.

Cranberry Jam

YIELD: 1½ CUPS • ACTIVE TIME: 5 MINUTES • TOTAL TIME: 1 HOUR

INGREDIENTS

½ lb. fresh cranberries

½ cup sugar

½ cup apple cider

2 (¼-inch) slices of ginger

1 teaspoon orange zest

½ teaspoon salt

1. Place all of the ingredients in a small saucepan and bring to a boil. Reduce the heat so that the mixture simmers until the cranberries have broken down, about 20 to 25 minutes.

2. Transfer the mixture to a Mason jar and refrigerate until completely cool.

Cheese Board with Cranberry Jam and Pickled Husk Cherries

YIELD: 6 TO 8 SERVINGS • ACTIVE TIME: 20 MINUTES • TOTAL TIME: 1½ HOURS

Freighting a board with a variety of cheeses and a few other seasonal bites is one of the best, and easiest, ways to get a gathering off on the right foot. The beauty of it is that it can be plated beforehand, allowing the cheese to come to room temperature and exhibit every flavor lurking within.

INGREDIENTS

½ cup champagne vinegar

½ cup water

½ cup sugar

1 teaspoon salt

½ cup husk cherries, husks removed

12 oz. blue cheese of choice

12 oz. hard-rind cheese of choice

12 oz. soft-rind cheese of choice

12 slices of bread, toasted

¼ cup Cranberry Jam (see sidebar)

¼ cup Apple Butter (see page 97)

½ cup roasted peanuts

2 oz. honeycomb

1 Place the vinegar, water, sugar, and salt in a small saucepan and bring to a boil. Remove from heat, let cool slightly, and then pour over the husk cherries. Cover and transfer the mixture to the refrigerator for at least 1 hour.

2 While the husk cherries are pickling, arrange the cheeses, toasted bread, Cranberry Jam, Apple Butter, peanuts, and honeycomb on a serving board. Let stand at room temperature.

3 Add the pickled husk cherries and serve.

Festive Fall Cheeseboard

YIELD: 4 TO 6 SERVINGS • ACTIVE TIME: 5 MINUTES • TOTAL TIME: 1 HOUR

Fall means watching football for many, and this lovely board allows you to please everyone without having to run around the kitchen all morning.

INGREDIENTS

Assorted fresh goat cheeses

Assorted aged cheeses

Charcuterie (such as hard salami, prosciutto, and speck)

Nuts, roasted (Marcona almonds and pecans work well)

Fresh or dried fruit (citrus, grapes, dried apricots, dates, figs, and currants are good options)

1 baguette or other crusty bread, sliced

Olives or cornichons

Honey

Jam

1 Take cheeses out of the fridge 1 hour prior to serving and allow them to come to room temperature.

2 Arrange ingredients on a serving board.

'Tis the Season for Cheesin' Holiday Board

YIELD: 4 TO 6 SERVINGS • ACTIVE TIME: 15 MINUTES
TOTAL TIME: 1 HOUR

The table can get a little crowded around the holidays, which means you've got to keep your board simple but still make it count.

1 Finely chop nuts, fruits, and/or fresh herbs as desired into a consistent blend.

2 Remove goat cheese log from packaging and roll or press into your finely chopped blend.

3 Allow to come to room temperature before arranging on the board with the remaining ingredients. If preparing in advance, wrap in plastic wrap and store in refrigerator for 1 to 2 days.

INGREDIENTS

½ cup roasted nuts, dried fruit, and/or fresh herbs to roll goat cheese in

4 oz. fresh goat cheese

Candied nuts

Chocolate truffles

Blackberries or other fresh fruit

Preserves and Other Condiments

Preserving fruits and vegetables was born out of necessity. Before refrigeration, the only way to consume berries, stone fruits, tomatoes, and the like out of season was in a jam, jelly, or preserve. There is a difference between the three. Jelly and jam are both made by crushing the main ingredient, but jelly only uses the juice yielded from the process, while jam includes pulp. The fruit or vegetable used in a preserve isn't crushed; instead the main ingredient is chopped up, cooked with sugar, and then stored in syrup or jam.

Made to be sweet, savory, or downright spicy, preserved fruits and vegetables are ideal additions to serving boards. Pairing them with other condiments adds balance and helps accentuate all the other flavors.

Fig Jam

YIELD: 3 TO 4 CUPS • ACTIVE TIME: 30 MINUTES
TOTAL TIME: 1 HOUR AND 15 MINUTES

Yes, the store has some decent options, but this fig jam is easy to make at home and you'll certainly taste the difference. It's perfect with scones, breads, and cheeses.

INGREDIENTS

2 lbs. figs, stemmed and cut into ½-inch pieces

1½ cups granulated sugar

¼ cup water

¼ cup lemon juice

Pinch of salt

1 vanilla bean, split and seeded (optional)

1 cinnamon stick (optional)

1 Place all of the ingredients in a medium saucepan and bring to a boil. Stir occasionally until the sugar is dissolved. If you include the vanilla bean in your preparation, add the seeds and the pod.

2 Reduce heat to low. Cook while stirring occasionally, for 30 to 60 minutes or until the liquid is thick, sticky, and falls heavily from the spoon.

3 Remove pan from heat and, if using, discard the vanilla pod and cinnamon stick.

4 For a chunky jam, gently mash the large pieces of fig with a fork or potato masher. For a smoother jam, process the mixture in a food processor.

5 Spoon jam into jars, leaving ¼-inch space at the top and cover with lid. Let cool to room temperature, then refrigerate. Store the jam in the refrigerator for up to 2 months.

Cranberry Preserves

YIELD: 2 CUPS • ACTIVE TIME: 15 MINUTES • TOTAL TIME: 45 MINUTES

These preserves are here to save your holidays, as they'll keep you clear of store-bought cranberry sauce.

1 Bring all ingredients to a boil in a large, heavy saucepan over medium heat, stirring occasionally.

2 Reduce heat. Simmer while stirring occasionally until the mixture thickens, about 20 minutes. Remove the saucepan from heat.

3 Force the mixture through a fine-mesh sieve into a bowl, discarding skins and seeds. Cool, while stirring occasionally. Serve when cooled to room temperature or store in the refrigerator for up to 4 days.

INGREDIENTS

1 (12 oz.) bag (about 3½ cups) fresh or frozen cranberries

1 cup sugar

½ cup fresh orange juice

1 cup water

Strawberry-Rhubarb Chutney

This tangy chutney is the best way to capture the end of the spring and the beginning of summer.

INGREDIENTS

2 tablespoons olive oil

¼ cup red onion, diced

2 garlic cloves, grated on a microplane

1-inch piece of ginger, minced or grated on a microplane

5 rhubarb stalks, thinly sliced to ¼-inch pieces

1 cup white wine

3 cardamom pods, seeded and ground

5 cloves, ground

1 teaspoon black ground pepper

¼ cup organic cane sugar

2 tablespoons lime juice

2 tablespoons apple cider vinegar

1 pint strawberries, diced

1 In a medium size pot, heat up olive oil and then sweat the red onions for about 1 minute. Add the garlic, ginger, and rhubarb. Sweat for about 3 to 5 mins on medium heat, stirring frequently.

2 Add the white wine to deglaze, then cook for about 1 minute. Add spices, sugar, lime juice, and vinegar and cook for another 2 to 5 minutes.

3 Once desired consistency for rhubarb is achieved add strawberries and cook for about 2 minutes. Check seasoning and adjust accordingly.

PRO TIP: IF YOU WOULD LIKE A SMOOTHER CHUTNEY, COOK FOR AN ADDITIONAL 5 TO 10 MINUTES ONCE THE STRAWBERRIES HAVE BEEN ADDED.

Quince Paste

This popular paste is Spanish in origin and goes particularly well with Manchego cheese.

1 Preheat oven to 350°F and lightly oil a 1-quart terrine.

2 Scrub quinces and pat dry. Place quinces in a small baking pan and cover with foil. Place in the middle rack of the oven. Bake until tender, about 2 hours.

3 Transfer the pan to a rack to cool. Once the quinces are cool enough to handle, peel, quarter, and core the quinces using a sharp knife.

4 In a food processor, puree the quinces with ¼ cup water until smooth. If the mixture is too thick, add the remaining water a little at a time as needed. Pass the puree through a large fine sieve into a liquid measuring cup. Transfer puree to a 3-quart heavy saucepan and add an equivalent amount of sugar.

5 Cook quince puree over moderate heat. Stir constantly until it thickens and starts to pull away from the side of the pan, about 25 minutes. Pour puree into a terrine, smooth the top with an offset spatula, and cool. Loosely cover in plastic wrap and chill until set, about 4 hours.

6 Run a knife around sides of terrine and invert quince paste onto a platter. Quince paste, if wrapped in waxed paper and plastic wrap, can be kept chilled for 3 months.

7 Slice paste before serving.

INGREDIENTS

4 medium quinces (about 2 lbs. total)

¼ to ½ cup water

2 to 3 cups sugar

Blood Orange Marmalade

YIELD: 6 CUPS • ACTIVE TIME: 20 MINUTES
TOTAL TIME: 1½ HOURS

This vibrant preserve adds color and considerable flavor to any serving board.

INGREDIENTS

2 lbs. blood oranges

3 tablespoons fresh lemon juice

4 cups sugar

1 Using vegetable peeler, carefully remove the peels from 3 or 4 oranges. Remove any white pith from the peels with a sharp knife. Cut peels into extremely thin slices and set aside.

2 Peel the remaining blood oranges and discard the peels. Remove the membranes and seeds from the oranges, then cut into small cubes.

3 In a 3-quart saucepan, place orange segments, lemon juice, and sugar. Bring to a boil over medium-high heat, stirring frequently. Once boiling, reduce heat to medium. Simmer for about 45 minutes until the mixture reaches 225°F on a candy thermometer.

4 Meanwhile, in a 1-quart saucepan, place orange peel slices and cover with water. Bring to a boil. Cook for about 4 minutes, then drain and set aside. Add the slices of peel to the larger saucepan during last few minutes of simmering.

5 Ladle marmalade into sterilized jars. Top with sterilized lids and rims.

6 Cool completely before storing.

Pantry Chutney

Any combination of dried fruit will work in this chutney, and it can likely be made with items you already have in your pantry.

1 Combine shallot, coriander, ginger, and oil in a medium saucepan and cook over medium heat until fragrant, about 1 minute.

2 Add apricots, vinegar, figs, prunes, raisins, molasses, and the water. Season with salt and pepper.

3 Bring to a simmer and cook until fruit is soft and the liquid is almost completely evaporated. If the mixture becomes too thick, you can add more water to thin it out. Let cool, cover, and store in the refrigerator for up to 1 week.

INGREDIENTS

1 shallot, diced

1 tablespoon coriander seeds

1 tablespoon ginger, peeled and diced

1 teaspoon vegetable oil

1½ cups dried apricots, coarsely chopped

1 cup apple cider vinegar

¼ cup dried figs, coarsely chopped

¼ cup prunes, coarsely chopped

¼ cup golden raisins

¼ cup dark molasses

1 ½ cups water

Kosher salt and freshly ground black pepper, to taste

Apricot and Chili Jam

YIELD: 8 CUPS • ACTIVE TIME: 20 MINUTES • TOTAL TIME: 1½ HOURS

This spicy jam pairs nicely with Brie, as well as a variety of goat cheeses.

INGREDIENTS

2 lbs. of apricots

Zest and juice from 1 small lemon

2 lbs. sugar

1 cup water

3 or 4 red chilies, according to taste

1 tablespoon unsalted butter or margarine

1 Wash and dry all of the apricots. Cut in half and remove the stones from the center. Slice the fruit into smaller pieces and add to a large saucepan. Add the lemon zest and juice, the sugar, and the water.

2 Dice the chilies. If desired, you can blend the chilies in a food processor instead. Add the chopped chilies and their seeds into the saucepan and mix with the apricots. Slowly bring the mixture to a boil.

3 Stir gently until all of the sugar has dissolved. Allow the mixture to hold a rapid boil for a few minutes.

4 Reduce the heat to a simmer and cook for 15 to 20 minutes, stirring constantly to prevent the mixture from burning. If you prefer a chunkier jam, make sure to stir gently so that the chunks of fruit stay intact. If you want a smoother jam, mash the mixture as you stir.

5 To test your jam, remove a spoonful and drop it onto a chilled saucer. If a skin doesn't begin to form after a minute, continue simmering and testing.

6 If the jam feels like a soft jelly and has started to form a thin skin, remove the pan from the heat. Add the butter and stir to disperse any froth. Cool for 15 minutes, then fill your sterilized glass jam jars. Allow to cool completely before storing in the refrigerator.

Apple Butter

YIELD: 3 CUPS . ACTIVE TIME: 25 MINUTES . TOTAL TIME: 2 HOURS

Despite the name, there is no butter in this preparation. Instead, the moniker refers to the texture, which is as smooth as butter. Be sure to include the skin and seeds of the apple, as they will enhance the flavor and help the mixture set.

1 Place the brandy in a saucepan over medium-high heat and cook until it has reduced by half. Remove from heat and set aside.

2 Make sure to wash apples thoroughly. Cut them into quarters, place them in a stockpot, and cover with cold water. Bring to a boil over medium-high heat and then reduce the heat so that the apples simmer. Cook until tender, about 15 minutes, and then drain.

3 Preheat the oven to 225°F. Run the apples through a food mill and catch the pulp in a mixing bowl. Add the reduced brandy and the remaining ingredients, stir to combine, and transfer to a shallow baking dish.

4 Place the dish in the oven and bake, while stirring the mixture every 10 minutes, until all of the excess water has evaporated, about 1 to 1½ hours. Remove from the oven, transfer the mixture to a food processor, and puree until smooth.

INGREDIENTS

3 cups brandy

5 lbs. apples

½ cup maple syrup

¼ cup brown sugar

1 teaspoon salt

½ teaspoon cinnamon

¼ teaspoon ground coriander

¼ teaspoon whole cloves

¼ teaspoon nutmeg

Flavored Honey

Infusing honey with herbs, vegetables, or flowers allows it to partner with any and all serving boards.

1 Whatever you choose to infuse the honey with, keep in mind that the smaller the pieces of it are, the more difficult it will be to strain out. For instance, if using herbs or flowers, use them whole or separate them into their stems, leaves, and/or buds.

2 Place infusing element in the bottom of a jar. Then, fill the jar almost to the top with honey. Using a chopstick or other implement, coat the infusing element with honey. Fill the jar with more honey, then wipe the rim with a clean cloth and cover tightly.

3 Let the mixture infuse for at least 5 days. If the infusing element floats to the top, turn the jar over to keep well coated. For a more intense flavor, infuse for up to 2 weeks.

4 Strain the honey into a clean jar. Depending on the volume of the mixture and the size of the strainer, you may need to do this in stages.

5 Secure the jar's lid tightly and store in a cool, dry place. It will last indefinitely.

INGREDIENTS

1 to 2 oz. dried herbs, vegetables, or flowers

1 cup honey

Green Tomato Jam

This savory jam is a great way to utilize an overabundance of green tomatoes and allow tomato season to be enjoyed any time of the year.

INGREDIENTS

3 lbs. green tomatoes

Zest and juice of 1 lemon

1 lb. sugar

1 Wash the tomatoes and pat dry. Remove the core, chop into small pieces, and remove the seeds. Place the tomato pieces in a large, nonreactive pot with a heavy bottom.

2 Keep the zest refrigerated in a small bowl with a small amount of lemon juice to keep it hydrated. Add the sugar and the juice from half the lemon in the pot. Toss, cover, and place in the refrigerator to macerate overnight.

3 In the morning, place the pot with the green tomatoes over medium-high heat. The tomatoes should have given off a fair amount of liquid overnight. Bring to a boil, stirring occasionally to avoid scorching.

4 Lower the heat so that the tomatoes are gently boiling, and cook for about an hour, stirring occasionally. Once the mixture pulls away from the pot's walls when stirred, remove from the heat and add the lemon zest.

5 With an immersion blender, puree the mixture

thoroughly. Alternatively, use a regular blender, mixing in small batches until fully combined.

6 Pour the jam into clean jars and allow to cool to room temperature. Seal and store in the refrigerator for up to 3 weeks, or in the freezer for up to 3 months.

Pikliz

This spicy, pickled vegetable slaw is a staple in Haitian cuisine, and is the perfect way to add a kick to your next spread.

1 Place the vegetables in a large mixing bowl and toss to combine.

2 Transfer the mixture to a large, sterilized Mason jar and press down on it. Add vinegar until the mixture is completely covered.

3 Cover with a lid and let the mixture sit for 1 day before using.

INGREDIENTS

4 habanero peppers, seeded and sliced

½ cup cabbage, grated

¼ cup carrot, grated

¼ cup green beans, chopped

¼ cup red bell pepper, sliced

½ cup shallots, sliced

½ cup white onion, sliced

White vinegar, as needed

Beer Mustard

This simple preparation brings out subtleties in cheeses and cured meats without overpowering them.

INGREDIENTS

2 cups yellow mustard seed

½ cup brown mustard seed

3 cups malt vinegar

4 cups beer

¾ cup honey

1 cup brown sugar

1 tablespoon salt

½ cup dry mustard

5 allspice berries, ground

½ cup Munich malt, ground

1 Place all ingredients in a large saucepan and cook over medium heat until the seeds are soft.

2 Transfer to a food processor and puree until it achieves the desired texture. Let cool before serving.

Cilantro-Mint Chutney

Typically served with Indian food, this chutney can be used to add a little zing to milder cheeses like mozzarella.

1 Place all ingredients in a blender and puree. Take care not to over-puree the mixture. You want the chutney to have some texture.

INGREDIENTS

2 cups fresh cilantro sprigs, packed

1 cup fresh mint leaves, packed

½ cup white onion, chopped

⅓ cup water

1 tablespoon lime juice

1 teaspoon green chili, chopped (serrano or Thai are good options; include the seeds or adjust to your taste)

1 teaspoon sugar

¾ teaspoon salt, or to taste

Mostarda

Perfect to serve alongside cured meat, this northern Italian condiment is made from candied fruit and a thick, mustard-flavored syrup.

INGREDIENTS

¼ lb. dried apricots, roughly chopped

¼ cup dried cherries, roughly chopped

1 shallot, minced

1½ teaspoons crystallized ginger, minced

½ cup dry white wine

3 tablespoons white wine vinegar

3 tablespoons water

3 tablespoons sugar

1 teaspoon dried mustard

1 teaspoon Dijon mustard

1 tablespoon unsalted butter

1 In a small saucepan, combine the apricots, cherries, shallot, ginger, wine, vinegar, water, and sugar and bring to a boil. Cover and cook over medium heat until all of the liquid is absorbed and the fruit is soft, about 10 minutes.

2 Stir in the dried mustard, Dijon mustard, and butter. Simmer until the mixture is jam-like, about 2 to 3 minutes.

3 Serve warm or at room temperature, or store in the refrigerator for up to 1 week.

Homemade Horseradish

YIELD: 1 CUP • ACTIVE TIME: 5 MINUTES • TOTAL TIME: 5 MINUTES

This spicy condiment can be served by itself or added to a variety of recipes to add a punch. It pairs perfectly with cured meat and a selection of subtle cheeses.

1 Place all of the ingredients in a blender or food processor and puree until smooth. Carefully remove the cover of the processor or blender, keeping your face away from the container.

2 Transfer to a jar, cover, and store in the refrigerator until ready to serve.

INGREDIENTS

1 cup horseradish root, peeled and chopped

¾ cup white vinegar

2 teaspoons white sugar

¼ teaspoon salt

Jalapeño Pepper Jam

If jalapeños aren't your favorite, feel free to substitute your preferred chili pepper. Should you want a mild jam, Anaheim peppers are a good choice.

INGREDIENTS

1 cup green bell pepper, seeded and minced or ground

¼ cup jalapeño pepper, seeded to taste and minced or ground

4 cups sugar

1 cup apple cider vinegar

1 (6 oz.) packet of liquid fruit pectin

3 to 5 drops of green food coloring (optional)

1 Combine peppers, sugar, and vinegar in a large nonreactive saucepan. Bring to a boil and cook for 5 minutes.

2 Remove from heat and let cool for 1 hour.

3 Add the pectin and the food coloring, if desired. Return to heat. Bring to a rolling boil and cook for 1 minute. Pour into hot, sterilized, half-pint canning jars, filling to within ½ inch of the top.

4 Wipe tops of the jars. Center lids on top and make sure to screw the bands on firmly.

5 Fill a canning kettle or a large pot with a bottom rack with water and bring to a boil. Gently lower jars into water. The water should cover the jars by at least 1 inch.

6 Bring water to a full boil. Reduce heat to a gentle boil, then cover and cook for 5 minutes.

7 Carefully remove the jars from the water using tongs or a jar-lifter.

8 Place upside down on a rack or thick towels and let cool without moving for 12 to 24 hours.

9 The jars will make popping sounds if sealed properly. Once cool, check the seal on each jar by pressing down on lid. If it doesn't push down, it's sealed. If it does push down, store in refrigerator. Otherwise, store in a cool, dark place for up to 1 year.

10 To serve, stir to soften. Then, pour over an 8 oz. block of cream cheese and spread on crackers.

TIP: THIS MUSTARD WILL KEEP FOR UP TO 6 MONTHS IF REFRIGERATED IN AN AIRTIGHT CONTAINER.

Garlic and Dill Mustard

Thanks to the garlic and dill, this simple mustard can dress up any charcuterie.

INGREDIENTS

For Brown Mustard:

½ cup mustard seeds

½ cup beer

⅓ cup water

1 tablespoon garlic, minced

1 tablespoon fresh dill, minced

3 tablespoons apple cider vinegar

1 tablespoon maple syrup

Water, as needed

For Yellow Mustard:

½ cup mustard seeds

½ cup white wine

1 tablespoon garlic, minced

1 tablespoon fresh dill, minced

⅓ cup white wine vinegar

1 tablespoon sugar

Water, as needed

1 Combine ingredients of chosen mustard in a stainless-steel bowl. Cover and let stand for 2 to 3 days.

2 Pour the mixture in a blender and blend until just a little grainy.

3 If the mustard is too thick, add water 1 tablespoon at a time until you reach your desired consistency.

Nuts, Olives, and Pickles

When most of us think of savory serving boards, we think of cured meats and creamy cheeses. But you need something to counter all that richness, which is where nuts, olives, and pickles come in. All three are a great way to inject a touch of lightness and different flavors into your spread, providing your board with a balance that will be welcomed by all.

Herb-Roasted Almonds

Roasted almonds stand alone great on their own, but are enhanced by the flavors imparted by the fresh herbs.

INGREDIENTS

½ teaspoon salt

1½ teaspoons water

2 cups whole raw almonds

3 sprigs fresh thyme, leaves only

1 sprig fresh savory, leaves only

2 teaspoons olive oil

1 Preheat oven to 375°F

2 Dissolve salt in water.

3 Add salt water to almonds and herbs.

4 Place almonds in single layer on sheet pan and roast for 15 to 20 minutes, stirring every 5 minutes. Once almonds brown remove them from the oven immediately.

5 Toss in olive oil and season to taste.

Maple Candied Walnuts

The sweet crunch of these snacks goes great with creamy cheeses and fatty cured meats.

1 Preheat oven to 375°F.

2 Melt butter in pan over medium heat. Stir in maple syrup and salt. Simmer for about 3 minutes, until mixture is frothy.

3 Add walnuts and coat, using a rubber spatula. Cook, stirring, for about 3 minutes.

4 Place walnuts in a single layer on a parchment-lined baking sheet and bake until walnuts are caramelized, about 10 minutes.

5 Stir and let cool and harden, about 30 minutes.

INGREDIENTS

1 tablespoon unsalted butter

⅓ cup maple syrup

⅛ teaspoon salt

2 cups walnut halves

Spiced Nut Mix

YIELD: 3 CUPS • ACTIVE TIME: 10 MINUTES • TOTAL TIME: 30 MINUTES

This recipe is wonderful for its flexibility, as it can handle any amount of spice.

INGREDIENTS

3 tablespoons unsalted butter

1 (15 to 16 oz.) can mixed nuts

¼ teaspoon Worcestershire sauce

½ teaspoon salt

¼ teaspoon paprika

¼ teaspoon cayenne pepper

¼ teaspoon chili powder

⅛ teaspoon ground cumin

1 In a large skillet, melt butter over low heat. Add nuts and Worcestershire sauce and cook, while stirring, for 5 to 7 minutes, or until the nuts are fragrant.

2 Remove the nuts with a slotted spoon and briefly let them drain on paper towels before transferring to a large bowl.

3 Combine remaining ingredients. Sprinkle over nuts and toss to coat. Set aside and let cool.

4 Let cool to room temperature before serving or storing in an airtight container.

Smoked and Spicy Almonds

YIELD: 2 CUPS • ACTIVE TIME: 10 MINUTES • TOTAL TIME: 45 MINUTES

These nuts can be stored in an airtight container for up to 1 month, but there's almost no chance they'll last that long.

1 Preheat oven to 350°F.

2 Line a baking sheet with parchment paper.

3 In a large bowl, combine butter, Worcestershire sauce, cumin, chili powder, garlic powder, onion powder, cayenne pepper, and salt.

4 Add almonds and toss to coat with butter mixture.

5 Transfer the almonds to the baking sheet and bake for 15 to 20 minutes, or until the almonds are golden brown and fragrant. Remove the sheet and flip the nuts regularly as they cook.

6 Remove from oven and let cool before serving or storing in an airtight container.

INGREDIENTS

4 tablespoons unsalted butter, melted

4 teaspoons Worcestershire sauce

1 teaspoon cumin

2 teaspoons chili powder

1 teaspoon garlic powder

½ teaspoon onion powder

1 teaspoon cayenne pepper

1 teaspoon salt

2 cups whole almonds

Chipotle Peanuts

YIELD: 1 CUP • ACTIVE TIME: 10 MINUTES • TOTAL TIME: 30 MINUTES

If you know your group loves milder cheeses, make sure these spicy treats make their way onto your board.

INGREDIENTS

1 cup peanuts, skins removed

1 teaspoon chipotle powder

⅛ teaspoon cayenne pepper

1 tablespoon lime juice

1 teaspoon lime zest

½ tablespoon vegetable oil

1 teaspoon salt

1 Preheat oven to 300°F. Place peanuts on a lined baking sheet and cook for 10 to 15 minutes, or until they are golden brown and fragrant.

2 Place the remaining ingredients in a bowl and stir until well combined. Add the peanuts and stir to combine.

3 Place on parchment paper to dry and cool.

Elevated Party Mix

YIELD: 12 CUPS • ACTIVE TIME: 15 MINUTES • TOTAL TIME: 1½ HOURS

A hot-and-spicy take on a bona fide classic. Don't be shy about substituting your favorites for what's suggested here.

INGREDIENTS

6 cups Chex cereal

1 cup pretzel twists or sticks

1 cup sesame sticks (typically found in the bulk food area at a health food or grocery store)

1 cup white cheddar cheese crackers

1 cup cashews

1 cup pecans

½ cup sesame seeds

¾ cup unsalted butter

1½ tablespoons soy sauce

2 teaspoons Garam Masala

2 teaspoons curry powder

1 teaspoon sugar

1 teaspoon cayenne pepper

1 Preheat oven to 250°F.

2 Line two baking sheets with parchment paper.

3 Combine Chex, pretzels, sesame sticks, crackers, nuts, and sesame seeds in a large bowl.

4 Place the remaining ingredients in a medium saucepan and cook over medium heat until the butter is melted.

5 Stir the butter mixture and then pour it over the cereal mixture. Stir until evenly coated.

6 Spread mixture onto prepared baking sheets and bake for 1 hour.

7 Remove from oven and let cool before serving. This mix will keep in an airtight container for 1 month.

Quick Pickles

YIELD: 2 PINTS • ACTIVE TIME: 15 MINUTES • TOTAL TIME: 12 HOURS TO 2 DAYS

This forgiving, flexible, and flavorful recipe allows you to pickle any vegetable, so long as it's fresh.

INGREDIENTS

1 lb. fresh vegetables, such as cucumbers, carrots, green beans, summer squash, or cherry tomatoes

2 sprigs fresh herbs, such as thyme, dill, or rosemary (optional)

1 to 2 teaspoons whole spices, such as black peppercorns, coriander, or mustard seeds (optional)

1 teaspoon dried herbs or ground spices (optional)

2 garlic cloves, smashed or sliced (optional)

1 cup vinegar, such as white, apple cider, or rice

1 cup water

1 tablespoon kosher salt or 2 teaspoons pickling salt

1 tablespoon granulated sugar (optional)

1 Wash 2 wide-mouth pint jars, lids, and bands in warm soapy water and rinse well. Set aside to dry, or dry by hand.

2 Wash and dry the vegetables. Peel carrots, if using. Trim the ends of the green beans, if using. Cut vegetables into desired shapes and sizes.

3 Divide whatever herbs, spices, and/or garlic you are using evenly between the jars.

4 Pack the vegetables into the jars, making sure there is a ½-inch of space remaining at the top. Pack them in as tightly as you can without damaging the vegetables.

5 Combine the vinegar, water, and salt in a small saucepan and cook over high heat. If using, add the sugar. Bring to a boil, stirring to dissolve the salt and sugar. Pour the brine over the vegetables, filling each jar to within ½-inch of the top. You may not use all the brine.

6 Gently tap the jars against the counter a few times to remove all the air bubbles. Top off with more pickling brine if necessary.

7 Place the lids on the jars and screw on the bands until tight.

8 Let the jars cool to room temperature. Store the pickles in the refrigerator. The pickles will improve with flavor as they age, so try to wait at least 48 hours before cracking them open.

Dilly Beans

YIELD: 5 PINTS • ACTIVE TIME: 10 MINUTES • TOTAL TIME: 1 WEEK

These crunchy and flavorful beans look great on any board. Be sure not to overcook them; you want to retain that crunch.

1 Prepare a boiling water bath and 5-pint jars. Place lids and bands in a small saucepan and simmer over low heat while you prepare the beans.

2 Wash and trim the beans so that they fit in jar. If you have particularly long beans, cut them in half. Combine vinegar, water, and salt in a medium saucepan and bring to a boil.

3 While the pickling liquid heats, pack your beans into the jars, leaving ½-inch of space free at the top.

4 Place 1 clove of garlic, 1 teaspoon dill seeds, and 1 teaspoon red pepper flakes in each jar.

5 Slowly pour the hot brine over the beans, leaving ½-inch from the top free. After the jars are full, use a wooden chopstick to remove the air bubbles. Add more brine if necessary.

6 Wipe the rims, apply lids and bands, and process in the hot water bath for 10 minutes. Let beans sit for at least 1 week before serving.

INGREDIENTS

3 lbs. green beans

2½ cups white vinegar

2½ cups water

4 tablespoons pickling salt

5 medium garlic cloves

5 teaspoons dill seeds (not dill weed)

5 teaspoons red pepper flakes

Pickled Okra

Okra, which is also known as ladies' fingers, pickles well and looks great piled up on a board.

INGREDIENTS

1 lb. okra, trimmed

4 small dried red chilies

2 fresh bay leaves

2 garlic cloves, halved

1 teaspoon dill seeds

1 teaspoon coriander seeds

1 teaspoon black peppercorns

1½ cups water

1½ cups cider vinegar

1½ tablespoons kosher salt

1 In a large saucepan, bring 6 cups of water to a boil. This will serve as your bath once the jars have been closed.

2 Pack the okra, chilies, bay leaves, and garlic cloves into 2 sterilized, 1-pint canning jars. Divide the dill seeds, coriander seeds, and peppercorns evenly between each jar.

3 In a medium saucepan, combine the water, vinegar, and salt and bring to a boil over high heat, stirring to dissolve the salt.

4 Pour the brine over the okra, leaving a ½ inch of space at the top. Apply the lids and bands.

5 Place the jars in the boiling water and boil for 10 minutes. Remove, let cool to room temperature, and serve immediately. The jars can be stored in a cool, dark place for up to 1 year. Refrigerate after opening.

Pickled Asparagus

YIELD: 6 PINTS • ACTIVE TIME: 15 MINUTES • TOTAL TIME: 1 WEEK

Get your hands on the freshest asparagus you can find; it makes a big difference in flavor.

1 Cut the asparagus to fit the length of whatever jars you're using, leaving 1/4-inch of space free at the top of the jars. Pack the asparagus into the jars as tightly as you can. Tuck the fresh dill weed inbetween the asparagus.

2 To make the brine, place all remaining ingredients into a medium saucepan and bring to a boil. Boil for 3 minutes.

3 Pour the hot brine into the jars, making sure to get some of the seeds and garlic in each jar. Leave 1/4-inch of space free at the top of each jar. Screw the lids on tightly.

4 Once the jars have cooled, refrigerate them for at least a week before eating. The asparagus can be stored in the refrigerator for around a month.

5 If you want to can these for long-term storage, immediately after pouring in the hot liquid and sealing the jars, process the jars in a boiling water bath for 10 minutes. Remove the jars and let them sit undisturbed for 24 hours before moving them. These will keep for up to a year.

INGREDIENTS

3 lbs. asparagus, woody ends removed

2 to 3 sprigs fresh dill weed

2½ cups white vinegar

2½ cups water

¼ cup pickling salt

1 tablespoon dill seeds

2 teaspoons coriander seeds

2 teaspoons mustard seeds

1 teaspoon allspice berries

2 tablespoons cane sugar

4 garlic cloves, minced

Pickled Beets

This recipe works with any type of beet, but candy-striped beets look fantastic pickled in the jar and even better on a board. Keep in mind that red will stain a serving board and your guests' fingers.

INGREDIENTS

4 lbs. beets

2½ cups white vinegar

1¼ cup water

1¼ cup sugar

1 teaspoon pickling salt

2 small onions, thinly sliced

1 Scrub and trim beets, leaving a small section of the stem. Bring water to boil in a large saucepan, add the beets, and reduce the heat to a simmer. Cook for 30 minutes, or until beets are tender. Remove and let beets cool. Rinse and quarter the beets, while taking care to preserve the stem. When served on a board, in a bowl, or in a nice pile, the stem is something to grab onto.

2 Place the vinegar, water, sugar, and salt in a Dutch oven, bring to a boil, and then add the beets and onions. Reduce heat and let simmer for 5 to 10 minutes.

3 Pour mixture into hot jars, packing tightly. Pour additional liquid over the beets and onions leaving about ½ inch of space free at the top. Wipe jars clean, attach lids, apply bands, and screw on until tight.

4 In a large saucepan, bring 6 cups of water to a boil. This will serve as the bath once the jars have been closed. Place the jars in the bath for 30 minutes and then turn off the heat and let the jars stand for 5 to 10 minutes.

Standard Pickle

Champagne vinegar or distilled vinegar works best in most contexts, but feel free to get wild and use other ones. This brine works for everything from onions and carrots to bacon. And yes, pickled bacon is as awesome as it sounds. You can basically pickle whatever you want with this solution.

1 Combine all ingredients in a saucepan and bring to a boil.

2 Add desired pickling ingredients to the brine. Allow the brine to return to a boil. Cook for 1 minute.

3 Remove the saucepan from heat and allow to cool to room temperature before serving.

INGREDIENTS

2 parts vinegar

1 part sugar

1 part water

Pickled Tomatoes

YIELD: ½ CUP • ACTIVE TIME: 10 MINUTES • TOTAL TIME: 12 HOURS

In the midst of tomato season, where there are too many to know what to do with, try pickling tomatoes. Pickle whole cherry tomatoes or sliced green ones—no matter what they add a vibrant bite and color to any serving board.

INGREDIENTS

4 tablespoons white wine vinegar

1½ teaspoons brown sugar

2 teaspoons salt

½ teaspoon garlic, minced

2 teaspoons mustard seeds

¼ teaspoon cracked peppercorns

1 teaspoon cumin

Cayenne pepper, to taste

¼ teaspoon turmeric

1½ tablespoons extra virgin olive oil

1 tomato, concasse and chopped (see sidebar)

1 Combine all ingredients except the tomato in a small saucepan. Bring to a simmer over medium heat.

2 Remove from heat and let cool.

3 Once cool, add chopped tomatoes, place in refrigerator, and allow to marinate for 12 hours.

TO CONCASSE A TOMATO:

1. BOIL ENOUGH WATER FOR A TOMATO TO BE SUBMERGED AND ADD A PINCH OF SALT. WHILE IT IS HEATING, PREPARE AN ICE BATH AND SCORE THE TOP OF THE TOMATO WITH A PARING KNIFE, TAKING CARE NOT TO CUT INTO THE FLESH OF THE TOMATO. PLACE THE TOMATO IN THE BOILING WATER FOR 30 SECONDS, OR UNTIL THE SKIN BEGINS TO BLISTER.

2. CAREFULLY REMOVE IT FROM THE BOILING WATER AND PLACE IT IN THE ICE BATH. ONCE THE TOMATO IS COOL, REMOVE IT FROM THE ICE BATH AND USE A PARING KNIFE TO PEEL THE SKIN OFF, STARTING AT THE SCORED TOP. CUT THE TOMATO INTO QUARTERS, REMOVE THE SEEDS, AND CUT ACCORDING TO INSTRUCTIONS.

Hot and Spicy Carrots

YIELD: 1 PINT • ACTIVE TIME: 10 MINUTES • TOTAL TIME: 45 MINUTES

If you really want to dress up your serving board, use heirloom carrots and take advantage of their assorted colors.

1 Combine all ingredients except the daikon and carrots in a saucepan and bring to a boil.

2 If canning, cut the daikon and carrots to fit the jars without crushing them. Add the carrots and daikon to the brine. Allow the brine to return to a boil. Cook for 1 minute.

3 Remove the saucepan from heat and allow to cool to room temperature before serving.

INGREDIENTS

1 cup unseasoned rice vinegar

1 teaspoon kosher or sea salt

2 tablespoons sugar, plus 2 teaspoons

1 cup water

½ lb. daikon, peeled

½ lb. large carrots, peeled

Retro Bread and Butter Pickles

YIELD: ½ CUP • ACTIVE TIME: 5 MINUTES
TOTAL TIME: 12 HOURS TO 1 WEEK

This wonderful recipe proves that a classic bread and butter pickle can steal the show on any board.

INGREDIENTS

½ **English hothouse cucumber or 2 Persian cucumbers, thinly sliced**

1 **small onion, thinly sliced**

2 **jalapeño peppers, thinly sliced**

4 **large sprigs fresh dill**

2 **tablespoons coriander seeds**

2 **tablespoons mustard seeds**

2 **teaspoons celery salt**

2 **cups distilled white vinegar**

1 **cup sugar**

2 **tablespoons kosher salt**

1 Pack cucumber slices, onion, jalapeños, dill sprigs, coriander seeds, mustard seeds, and celery salt into a 1-quart jar.

2 Bring vinegar, sugar, and salt to a boil in a medium saucepan, stirring to dissolve sugar and salt. Carefully pour into jar, filling all the way to the top. Seal jar and refrigerate for at least 12 hours and up to 1 week.

Pickled Peppers

If you use a variety of chili peppers, this recipe is another great way to add color to your board.

1 In a large skillet, warm the oil over medium-high heat and add the chilies and garlic. Sauté, stirring frequently until softened, for about 5 minutes. Remove from heat and let the chilies cool until they can be handled.

2 Add the chilies and garlic to a sanitized 1-quart jar or 4 smaller mason jars. If desired, slice some of the chilies in half lengthwise in order to infuse the vinegar.

3 Place the vinegar, water, sugar, and salt in a small saucepan and cook, while stirring, until the sugar and salt are dissolved.

4 Pour the brine mixture over the chilies and allow the contents of the jar to cool to room temperature. Seal the jar and refrigerate for up to 1 month.

INGREDIENTS

2 tablespoons grapeseed oil

9 chilies of choice, assorted

4 garlic cloves, halved

1¾ cups white vinegar

¾ cup water

1 tablespoon sugar

½ teaspoon salt

Dips and Spreads

Dips and spreads are about as versatile as it gets. Whether you're an omnivore, vegan, or gluten-free, there are countless tasty preparations that fit any and all dietary requirements and tastes. It doesn't matter if you're using sliced vegetables, crackers, or bread, any of these dips and spreads can complement the contents of a serving board, or serve as the centerpiece.

Black Olive Tapenade

YIELD: 1½ CUP • ACTIVE TIME: 5 MINUTES • TOTAL TIME: 5 MINUTES

This spread can be made with any type of olives, but black olives are the most pleasing to the eye.

INGREDIENTS

1½ cups brine-cured olives, pitted,

1 teaspoon anchovy paste or 2 anchovy filets, minced

3 tablespoons capers, rinsed

1½ tablespoons fresh parsley, chopped

3 garlic cloves (roasting optional)

3 tablespoons lemon juice

¼ teaspoon black pepper, plus more to taste

¼ cup olive oil

Salt, to taste

1 In a food processor, combine olives, anchovy component, capers, parsley, garlic, lemon juice, and black pepper. Pulse 2 to 3 times until coarsely chopped.

2 Drizzle in olive oil and pulse a few more times until a chunky paste forms, scraping down the sides as needed.

3 Season to taste with salt and pepper and serve at room temperature.

Sun-Dried Tomato and Pistachio Tapenade

YIELD: 1½ TO 2 CUPS • ACTIVE TIME: 5 MINUTES • TOTAL TIME: 15 MINUTES

Everyone knows sun-dried tomatoes are divine, but pairing their sweetness with salty pistachios takes them to the next level.

INGREDIENTS

¼ cup extra virgin olive oil, plus one tablespoon

1 shallot, minced

1 teaspoon dry vermouth

¾ cup sun-dried tomatoes packed in oil

½ cup pistachios, shelled

½ cup fresh Italian parsley, chopped

1 teaspoon fresh thyme, minced

Zest and juice from ½ lemon

1 teaspoon sea salt

1 teaspoon freshly ground black pepper

Water, as needed

1 Place the 1 tablespoon of olive oil in a sauté pan and warm over medium heat. Add the shallot and cook until light brown, about 3 to 5 minutes.

2 Deglaze pan with vermouth. Remove from heat and let cool.

3 Place all ingredients into a food processor and puree until well combined. If too thick, add water 1 teaspoon at a time until the mixture reaches the desired consistency.

Whipped Herb Butter

YIELD: ½ CUP • ACTIVE TIME: 10 MINUTES • TOTAL TIME: 10 MINUTES

Chances are you've been blown away by an herb butter at a fancy restaurant. This recipe brings it well within your reach.

INGREDIENTS

1 tablespoon extra virgin olive oil

1 garlic clove

1 tablespoon fresh thyme, chopped

1 tablespoon fresh basil, chopped

1 stick unsalted butter

1 Place the olive oil and garlic in a food processor and puree until the garlic is finely chopped. Add the thyme and basil and blend until the herbs have colored the oil.

2 Using the whisk attachment on your hand-mixer, place the butter in the work bowl and whip at medium speed until it softens and lightens in color, about 5 minutes.

3 Add the herb oil to the butter and beat for 1 minute, or until combined.

4 Remove butter and place in the refrigerator until ready to serve.

Edamame Hummus

Edamame—young, green soybeans—add a sweet dimension to this hummus.

1 Place all ingredients in a blender and puree until smooth.

2 To serve, drizzle with extra virgin olive oil and top with toasted pine nuts.

INGREDIENTS

4 cups chickpeas

2 cups of edamame

½ cup water

¾ cup extra virgin olive oil, plus more for garnish

2 tablespoons salt

2 tablespoons tahini

3 garlic cloves

Toasted pine nuts, for garnish

Yogurt Dip

Artichokes, grilled cabbage, and anything savory are a good match for this tangy dip.

INGREDIENTS

1 cup plain yogurt

2 tablespoons cumin

Black pepper, to taste

Juice of 2 lemons

3 tablespoons olive oil

2 sprigs fresh dill, chopped

1 Place all ingredients in a bowl and stir until well combined. Refrigerate until ready to serve.

Strawberry Salsa

Strawberries in salsa? Don't knock it till you've tried it.

1 Place all ingredients in a bowl and stir until combined. Serve immediately.

INGREDIENTS

1 pint strawberries, diced

½ cup fresh cilantro, chopped

¼ cup fresh mint, chopped

1 shallot, minced

½ English cucumber, diced

1 jalapeño pepper, minced

Mike's Hot Honey Mustard Dip

YIELD: ½ CUP • ACTIVE TIME: 5 MINUTES • TOTAL TIME: 5 MINUTES

This specialty honey used to be tough to track down, but is increasingly available across the country.

INGREDIENTS

½ cup mayonnaise

2 tablespoons Dijon mustard

2 tablespoons Mike's Hot Honey

1 tablespoon lemon juice

Salt, to taste

1 Place all of the ingredients in a bowl and stir to combine. Season with salt and serve immediately.

Chipotle and Adobo Crema

YIELD: 1 CUP • ACTIVE TIME: 5 MINUTES • TOTAL TIME: 5 MINUTES

Serve this smoky sauce with crudité for a burst of flavor. Be warned: this sauce is addictive.

1 Place all ingredients in a bowl and stir until well combined. Add additional chipotle and honey to taste.

2 Garnish with cilantro and serve with pita chips, crudité, and charcuterie.

INGREDIENTS

8 oz. plain Greek yogurt

1 tablespoon Dijon mustard

1 tablespoon adobo sauce

1 chipotle in adobo, minced, plus more to taste

1 tablespoon honey, plus more to taste

Fresh cilantro, for garnish

Pita chips, crudité, and charcuterie, to serve

Black Bean Spread

Don't trust the subdued appearance of this spread, as it is exploding with flavor.

INGREDIENTS

2 (15 oz.) cans black beans

¼ cup tahini

¾ cup lime juice

¾ cup extra virgin olive oil

2 teaspoons sea salt

1 tablespoon freshly ground black pepper

1 teaspoon Tabasco®

1 teaspoon anchovy paste

Water, as needed

Fresh cilantro leaves, chopped, for garnish

Pita triangles and cruidté, to serve

1 Place all ingredients in a food processor and blend until desired consistency. If too thick, add a tablespoon of water. If too thin, add more black beans.

2 Garnish with cilantro and serve with warm pita triangles and crudité.

Sunchoke Aioli

The nutty, slightly savory flavor of sunchokes gets showcased perfectly in this spread.

1 In a small saucepan, add the sunchokes and cover with water.

2 Boil for 20 to 25 minutes, or until the interior flesh is very tender.

3 Remove from boiling water and submerge in ice water. Remove, cut sunchokes in half, and remove meat with a spoon.

4 Mash the sunchoke meat with a fork. Add the egg yolks, garlic, mustard, and lemon juice and whisk vigorously until the mixture is nice and smooth.

5 Slowly drizzle in the oil, whisking constantly. Season with salt and pepper, and serve.

INGREDIENTS

2 sunchokes

2 egg yolks

½ garlic clove, minced

½ teaspoon Dijon mustard

1 teaspoon lemon juice

½ cup extra virgin olive oil

Salt and pepper, to taste

Chicken Skin Butter

YIELD: ½ CUP • ACTIVE TIME: 15 MINUTES • TOTAL TIME: 30 MINUTES

Once you try this butter, you're certain to think up 100 pairings to go with it.

INGREDIENTS

Skin from 2 large chicken thighs

Flaky sea salt, to taste

½ cup unsalted butter, at room temperature

½ teaspoon fresh chives, chopped

1 Preheat the oven to 400°F.

2 Lay the chicken skin on a cutting board, skin-side down, and use a small, sharp knife to scrape off any excess fat and meat.

3 Stretch the skins out on a parchment-lined baking sheet and sprinkle with flaky sea salt.

4 Lay a second sheet of parchment paper over the skins and place a second baking sheet on top. Place both trays in the oven for 10 minutes, until the skins are golden and crisp. Remove and let the skins cool.

5 Once cooled, chop the skin into small, fine pieces. Add the butter and skin to a bowl and whisk until combined. Fold in the chives and serve.

Creamy Crudité Dip

This creamy and zesty dip goes with everything!

1 Combine all ingredients in a food processor except for the blue cheese. Add blue cheese and take care not to overmix to maintain the chunky texture. Refrigerate until ready to serve.

INGREDIENTS

1½ cups mayonnaise

2 cups sour cream

1 tablespoon fresh parsley, chopped

1 tablespoon fresh tarragon, chopped

1 tablespoon fresh chives, chopped

1 tablespoon fresh basil, chopped

1 tablespoon red wine vinegar

1 tablespoon sugar

1 teaspoon garlic powder

1 tablespoon Worcestershire sauce

Cracked pepper and kosher salt, to taste

1 (6 oz.) blue cheese of choice

Raita

This refreshing Indian specialty can help balance some of the spicier spreads on your board.

INGREDIENTS

½ cup plain yogurt

½ English cucumber, seeded and diced

¼ cup fresh cilantro, chopped

2 scallions, minced

¼ teaspoon coriander

½ teaspoon sea salt

½ teaspoon freshly ground black pepper

1 Place all ingredients in a bowl and stir until well combined. Refrigerate for 1 hour before serving.

Pork Pâté (aka Gorton)

YIELD: 10 TO 15 SERVINGS • ACTIVE TIME: 20 MINUTES • TOTAL TIME: 24 HOURS

This French-Canadian delicacy is a great way to balance a sweet board with a hint of savory. Pair this with some Purple Potato Chips (see page 15) and voilà! Your board is fit for a feast.

1 Preheat the oven to 300°F.

2 Place all of the ingredients in a Dutch oven and stir to combine. Cover, and cook over low heat until the pork falls apart at the touch of a fork, about 3 to 4 hours.

3 Remove from heat, discard the bay leaves, and transfer the pork shoulder to a plate. When the pork shoulder has cooled slightly, shred it with a fork.

4 Place the shredded pork and ½ cup of the juices from the pot in a blender. Puree until it forms a paste, adding more of the juices as needed.

5 Season with salt and pepper, transfer the paste to a large jar, and then pour the remaining juices over it. Cover the jar and store it in the refrigerator overnight before serving.

INGREDIENTS

1 (3- to 5-lb.) bone-in pork shoulder

3 onions, sliced

2 teaspoons ground cloves

1 tablespoon salt, plus more to taste

4 fresh bay leaves

2 teaspoons black pepper, plus more to taste

1 teaspoon nutmeg

Fava Bean Spread

YIELD: 4 CUPS • ACTIVE TIME: 20 MINUTES • TOTAL TIME: 35 MINUTES

This spread is packed with vitamins and flavor, so don't be scared off by the need to shell the fava beans.

INGREDIENTS

4 cups fava beans in the shell

½ to 1 cup olive oil

15 garlic cloves

5 tablespoons fresh rosemary, chopped

½ cup water

Salt and pepper, to taste

1 Bring water to boil in a medium saucepan. Shell the fava beans, add them to the saucepan, and cook for 1 to 2 minutes. Submerge in cold water and then remove the skins.

2 Heat ½ cup of oil in a large skillet over low heat. Add the fava beans and cook, while stirring, until tender. Set the beans aside.

3 In the same pan, add the garlic and cook until golden, adding oil as needed. Add rosemary and cook while stirring for 2 minutes, or until fragrant.

4 Working in four batches, place all ingredients in a food processor and puree until smooth. Make sure not to overprocess.

5 Adjust seasoning to taste and serve.

Traditional Hummus

YIELD: 1⅓ CUPS • ACTIVE TIME: 10 MINUTES • TOTAL TIME: 15 TO 20 MINUTES

Relying on store-bought varieties of hummus can sink a whole serving board. Luckily, this version is here to save the day.

1 If using canned chickpeas, drain the chickpeas into a strainer, reserving the liquid from the can. If time allows, remove the skins from each of the chickpeas. This will make your hummus much smoother.

2 Place the chickpeas, olive oil, tahini, lemon juice, garlic, salt, and pepper in a food processor.

3 Puree hummus until it is very smooth, about 5 to 10 minutes. Scrape down the sides of the bowl as needed to integrate any large chunks.

4 Adjust seasonings to taste. If the hummus is stiffer than desired, add 2 to 3 tablespoons of the reserved chickpea liquid and blend until ideal consistency is achieved.

5 Scrape the hummus into a bowl and serve with pita or vegetables.

INGREDIENTS

1 (15 oz.) can chickpeas or 2 cups drained, cooked chickpeas

3 tablespoons extra virgin olive oil

3 tablespoons tahini

1½ tablespoons lemon juice, plus more as needed

1 small garlic clove, roughly chopped

1 teaspoon salt

½ teaspoon finely ground black pepper

Pita or vegetables, to serve

Roasted Beet Spread

YIELD: 2 CUPS • ACTIVE TIME: 20 MINUTES • TOTAL TIME: 1½ HOURS

Roasting brings the best out of beets. The combination of this spread and goat cheese can't be beat.

INGREDIENTS

4 beets, peeled and cubed

¼ cup extra virgin olive oil

½ teaspoon sea salt, plus more to taste

¾ teaspoon cumin seeds

¾ teaspoon coriander seeds

2 teaspoons minced garlic (about 2 cloves), plus more to taste

2 teaspoons green chili, ribbed, seeded, and minced, plus more to taste

2 teaspoons lemon juice, plus more to taste

⅓ cup fresh cilantro leaves, minced

1 Preheat the oven to 400°F.

2 Line a baking sheet with parchment paper. Place the beets in a bowl with 2 tablespoons of the olive oil and ¼ teaspoon of salt. Toss to coat.

3 Arrange the beets on the baking sheet in a single layer and roast for about 1 hour, tossing periodically, until the beets are tender. You should have about 2 cups.

4 Heat the cumin and coriander seeds in a dry skillet over medium-high heat for about 2 minutes, stirring constantly, until they release their fragrance and change color slightly. Be careful not to burn them or they will become bitter.

5 Grind the seeds in a spice grinder or crush with a mortar and pestle.

6 Place the beets into a high-speed blender or food processor and add the remaining olive oil and salt, the ground seeds, garlic, chili, and lemon juice. Puree until well combined.

7 Adjust the garlic, chili, lemon juice, and salt to taste. Transfer the dip to a bowl, stir in the cilantro, and serve.

Taramasalata

A rich and salty Greek classic that will transport you to the shores of the Aegean. It goes particularly well with Sea Salt and Herb Crackers (see page 11).

1 Soak bread in water, then squeeze out excess water. Place all ingredients except oil in a food processor. Puree until smooth, gradually adding the oil until the desired texture is achieved.

2 Place in a serving dish and chill for 2 to 3 hours. Garnish with olives and parsley and serve with pita and vegetables.

INGREDIENTS

10 slices stale white bread, crusts removed

4 oz. fish roe

Juice of 2 lemons

1 small red onion, grated

¾ cup extra virgin olive oil

Olives, for garnish

Fresh parsley, for garnish

Pita and vegetables, to serve

White Bean and Rosemary Spread

YIELD: 2 CUPS • ACTIVE TIME: 5 MINUTES • TOTAL TIME: 45 MINUTES

Once you procure some fresh rosemary, this spread can be made from ingredients that are always on hand.

INGREDIENTS

2 cups cooked white beans or 1 (15 oz.) can white beans, rinsed and drained

2 tablespoons olive oil

2 teaspoons balsamic vinegar

2 garlic cloves, minced

1 tablespoon fresh rosemary, minced

⅓ cup celery, minced

Salt and freshly ground black pepper, to taste

2 pinches of red pepper flakes (optional)

Sesame seeds, for garnish (optional)

1 Place the beans in a bowl, and mash about half of them with a fork. Add the olive oil, vinegar, garlic, rosemary, and celery and toss well.

2 Season with salt, pepper, and red pepper flakes, if desired.

3 Cover. Let stand for about 30 minutes and season to taste before serving. If refrigerated, allow to come to room temperature before serving.

Chickpea Spread

The addition of cilantro separates this spread from a traditional hummus.

1 Mince the garlic in a food processor.

2 Add the cilantro and pulse until combined.

3 Add the remaining ingredients and puree until smooth. Add additional water as needed to reach the desired consistency, and serve.

INGREDIENTS

2 garlic cloves

½ bunch fresh cilantro, stems removed

1 (15 oz.) can chickpeas, rinsed and drained

Zest and juice of 2 lemons

¾ cup tahini

4 tablespoons water, plus more as needed

4 tablespoons olive oil

2 teaspoons salt

½ teaspoon pepper

Roasted Pumpkin Dip

YIELD: 2 CUPS • ACTIVE TIME: 5 MINUTES • TOTAL TIME: 35 MINUTES

Pumpkins are king once the weather gets cold. Their sweet, savory flavor is reminiscent of a warm fire on a crisp fall day.

INGREDIENTS

1 medium sugar pumpkin

1 tablespoon vegetable oil

2 teaspoons sea salt

1 teaspoon freshly ground black pepper

¼ cup extra virgin olive oil

1 teaspoon fresh thyme leaves, minced

¼ teaspoon freshly ground nutmeg

¼ cup Parmesan cheese, grated

1 tablespoon lemon juice

1 tablespoon plain Greek yogurt or sour cream

1 Preheat the oven to 425°F. Cut the pumpkin in half, discard the seeds, brush it with the vegetable oil, and sprinkle with 1 teaspoon of the salt. Place on a baking sheet and bake for 25 to 30 minutes. Remove and let cool.

2 Scrape insides from the pumpkin and place in a food processor. Add the remaining ingredients and blend until smooth. Serve immediately.

TIP: SUBSTITUTING ROASTED BUTTERNUT SQUASH FOR THE PUMPKIN MAKES THE PERFECT FALL SPREAD.

Green Hummus

Acquiring its vivid green color from an array of fresh herbs, this hummus brightens up any serving board.

INGREDIENTS

¼ cup tahini

¼ cup lemon juice

2 tablespoons olive oil, plus more for serving

¼ cup fresh parsley, chopped

¼ cup fresh cilantro, chopped

2 jalapeño peppers, seeded, stemmed, and chopped

3 green onions, chopped, plus more for garnish

2 garlic cloves, minced

½ teaspoon salt, plus more to taste

1 (15 oz.) can chickpeas, drained and rinsed

1 to 2 tablespoons water, as needed

Fresh herbs, chopped, for garnish (optional)

1 Add the tahini and lemon juice to a food processor and puree for about 1 minute. Use a plastic spatula to scrape down the sides of the bowl, if needed.

2 Add olive oil, parsley, cilantro, jalapeños, green onion, garlic, and salt. Puree for about 1 minute, scraping down the bowl as necessary.

3 Add the chickpeas and puree until the hummus has a thick and smooth texture, about 1 to 2 minutes. Scrape down the bowl a few times while pureeing.

4 If hummus is too thick, puree and slowly add 1 to 2 tablespoons water until it reaches the desired consistency.

5 Transfer the hummus into a small serving bowl. Drizzle a tablespoon of olive oil on top and garnish with the additional green onions and herbs, if using.

6 Serve or store in an airtight container and refrigerate for up to 1 week.

Trout Pâté

YIELD: 4 CUPS • ACTIVE TIME: 10 MINUTES • TOTAL TIME: 10 MINUTES

This pâté is dynamite on toasted pieces of baguette and crackers.

INGREDIENTS

8 oz. cream cheese

8 oz. crème fraîche

1 cup shallots, minced

1 cup fresh chives, minced

4 oz. lemon juice

3 teaspoons kosher salt

2¼ cups smoked trout

1 Place the cream cheese and crème fraîche into the bowl of a standing mixer and turn on low. Mix until combined.

2 Add the shallots, chives, lemon juice, and salt. Continue to mix on low.

3 Add smoked trout and increase speed until the meat is shredded but not pulverized.

4 Scoop from mixing bowl and serve.

Baba Ganoush

Roasting the eggplants is a must for this spread, as it draws out their meaty flavor.

1 Preheat oven to 375°F. Cut eggplants in half and poke holes over the surface using a fork. Place in a bowl and toss with 1 to 2 tablespoons of olive oil and the salt. Place the eggplants flesh-side up on a baking sheet and bake for 15 to 20 minutes until lightly brown and tender all the way through.

2 Remove eggplant from the oven and allow to cool slightly. Once cool enough to handle, remove skins and discard.

3 Place the eggplant in a food processor with the remaining ingredients and pulse until smooth but textured.

4 Serve immediately or refrigerate until ready to use.

INGREDIENTS

3 medium eggplants

½ cup extra virgin olive oil

1 teaspoon sea salt

1 tablespoon tahini

½ teaspoon chili powder

Juice of 2 lemons

1 garlic clove, grated

1 teaspoon freshly ground black pepper

Roasted Artichoke and Garlic Spread

YIELD: 1 CUP • ACTIVE TIME: 5 MINUTES • TOTAL TIME: 10 TO 20 MINUTES

Pairing the nutty flavor of artichokes with the sweetness of roasted garlic makes for an incredibly versatile spread.

INGREDIENTS

1 (12 oz.) bag frozen artichoke hearts, thawed and halved or quartered

4 garlic cloves, peeled

2 tablespoons white vinegar or apple cider vinegar

¼ teaspoon salt

4 tablespoons olive oil

Pinch of onion powder (optional)

1 Spread the artichoke hearts and garlic on a cookie sheet and broil for 5 to 15 minutes, until browned.

2 Combine all ingredients in a blender or food processor and puree until desired texture is achieved.

3 The spread can be eaten warm immediately or covered and chilled. Serve with bread, use as a sandwich or wrap filling, or use as a dip.

Karla's Guacamole

YIELD: 2 CUPS • ACTIVE TIME: 10 MINUTES • TOTAL TIME: 10 MINUTES

This guacamole recipe has the perfect balance between creamy avocado and delectable seasonings and is perfect with tortilla chips.

1 In a large bowl, add the avocados and mash roughly.

2 Coat the avocados with lime juice. Add the tomatoes, onion, garlic, salt, pepper, and Old Bay seasoning.

3 Fold ingredients together until mixture reaches the desired consistency. While a chunkier guacamole is easier for dipping, pureeing the mixture in a food processor gives it a smoother finish.

4 Garnish with cilantro. Finish with a final splash of lime juice and serve.

INGREDIENTS

3 avocados, halved, seeded, and peeled

Juice of 2 to 3 limes, plus more for garnish

2 Roma tomatoes, seeded and diced

1 medium red onion, diced

1 to 2 garlic cloves, minced

½ teaspoon salt

Pepper, to taste

Old Bay seasoning, to taste

1 tablespoon fresh cilantro, chopped, for garnish

Bigger Bites

The serving board is a wonderful culinary pasture through which the hungry may graze as they sip drinks, chat, and enjoy the moment. But even the most bountiful collection of little bites will leave some wanting more. Fear not, this chapter proves that the serving board can take on snacks of all sizes, from skewers and tempura to delectable salads.

Greek Couscous and Shrimp Salad

YIELD: 6 SERVINGS • ACTIVE TIME: 40 MINUTES • TOTAL TIME: 50 MINUTES

This light, shrimp-packed salad will have you going back for seconds.

INGREDIENTS

For the Shrimp

¾ lb. shrimp (16/20, shell on preferred)

6 bunches fresh mint

10 garlic cloves, peeled

For the Salad

3½ cups chicken stock

3 cups toasted Israeli couscous

1 bunch of asparagus, bottom 2 inches removed

3 Roma tomatoes, diced

2 tablesoons fresh mint, chopped

1 tablespoon fresh oregano, chopped

½ English cucumber, diced

Zest and juice of 1 large lemon

½ cup red onion, diced

½ cup sun-dried tomatoes, sliced thin

¼ cup pitted kalamata olives, chopped

⅓ cup greek olive oil or extra virgin olive oil

½ cup feta cheese

Salt and pepper, to taste

1 Place the shrimp, mint, and garlic in a stockpot and cover with water. Cook over medium heat until shrimp are cooked through. The shrimp should be firm and pink when done. Remove the shrimp from the pot, chill in the refrigerator, peel, and cut in half lengthwise. Set aside.

2 To make the salad, in a large stockpot, bring chicken stock to a boil and add the couscous. Reduce the heat to a simmer. Cover and cook for 7 to 10 minutes. Strain and chill the couscous immediately to avoid overcooking.

3 Fill the pot back up with water and bring to a boil. Add the asparagus and cook for 1 to 1½ minutes until it has softened a bit. Quickly strain in a colander and cover with ice cubes to stop the cooking process. This will keep the asparagus green and firm. Chop the asparagus into bite-sized pieces.

4 Add all the remaining ingredients, besides the feta and the shrimp, to a salad bowl. Add the couscous and asparagus and stir to combine. Top with the shrimp and the feta and serve.

TIP: YOU CAN BUY COUSCOUS PRE-TOASTED, BUT IF YOU ARE LOOKING TO BRING YOUR DISH TO THE NEXT LEVEL, TOAST YOUR COUSCOUS IN THE OVEN AT 375°F FOR 10 TO 12 MINUTES ON A BAKING SHEET. THIS WILL ADD A DELIGHTFUL NUTTY FLAVOR TO THE DISH.

Oyster Sliders

YIELD: 4 SERVINGS • ACTIVE TIME: 30 MINUTES
TOTAL TIME: 1 HOUR AND 15 MINUTES

The cornmeal crust on the bivalves and the red pepper mayo will convert anyone who claims not to like oysters.

1 Preheat the oven to 400°F.

2 Place the red peppers on a baking sheet and bake, turning occasionally, for 35 to 40 minutes, until blistered all over. Remove from the oven and let cool. Once cool enough to handle, remove the skins and seeds and set the flesh aside.

3 Place the oil in a Dutch oven and bring it to 350°F over medium-high heat. Place the cornmeal and salt in a bowl and stir to combine.

5 When the oil is ready, dip the oyster meat into the beaten eggs and the cornmeal-and-salt mixture. Repeat until evenly coated.

6 Place the oysters in the Dutch oven and fry until golden brown, about 3 to 5 minutes. Remove from the oil and set on a paper towel–lined plate to drain.

7 Place the butter in a skillet and melt over medium heat. Place the buns in the skillet and toast until lightly browned. Remove and set aside.

8 Place the roasted peppers and mayonnaise in a blender and puree until smooth. Spread the red pepper mayonnaise on the buns, add the fried oysters, and serve.

INGREDIENTS

3 red bell peppers

1 cup canola oil

1 cup cornmeal

Salt, to taste

½ lb. oyster meat

2 eggs, beaten

1 tablespoon unsalted butter

4 King's Hawaiian Rolls

½ cup mayonnaise

Southern Deviled Eggs

YIELD: 6 EGGS • ACTIVE TIME: 15 MINUTES • TOTAL TIME: 30 MINUTES

Deviled eggs are typically associated with the 1950s, but this version shows that they are a timeless treat.

INGREDIENTS

6 eggs

2 tablespoons yellow mustard

2 tablespoons mayonnaise

2 teaspoons whole grain mustard

2 cornichons, diced

2 teaspoons pimentos

Salt and pepper, to taste

5 sprigs fresh parsley, chopped, for garnish

1 sprig fresh dill, for garnish

1 slice of Spam, cut into triangles and fried, for garnish (optional)

1 Hard-boil the eggs and let cool. Remove the yolks.

2 Combine yolks in a small bowl with yellow mustard, mayonnaise, whole grain mustard, cornichons, and pimentos. Season with salt and pepper to taste.

3 Spoon yolk mixture delicately into each egg white shell.

4 Garnish with parsley, dill, and, if using, Spam.

Fontina Jalapeño Hush Puppies

YIELD: 4 TO 6 SERVINGS • ACTIVE TIME: 15 MINUTES • TOTAL TIME: 30 MINUTES

This Southern classic takes a delicious detour through the Southwest thanks to the jalapeño.

INGREDIENTS

2 cups vegetable oil

½ cup cornmeal

3 tablespoons all-purpose flour, plus 1½ teaspoons

4½ tablespoons sugar

¾ teaspoon salt

¼ teaspoon baking powder

⅛ teaspoon baking soda

⅛ teaspoon cayenne pepper

¼ cup buttermilk

1 egg, beaten

2 tablespoons jalapeño pepper, seeded and chopped

¾ cup fontina cheese, grated

1 Place oil in a Dutch oven and heat to 320°F.

2 Add the cornmeal, flour, sugar, salt, baking powder, baking soda, and cayenne pepper to a small bowl and whisk until combined.

3 In a separate bowl, add the buttermilk, egg, and jalapeño. Whisk to combine.

4 Combine the buttermilk mixture and the dry mixture.

5 Add the cheese and stir until combined.

6 Drop spoonfuls of the batter into the hot oil and fry until golden brown.

7 Remove from oil with a slotted spoon and place on paper towels to drain.

Tempura Broccoli

YIELD: 4 TO 6 SERVINGS • ACTIVE TIME: 10 MINUTES • TOTAL TIME: 20 MINUTES

Even those who recoil at the thought of broccoli will be unable to turn down this fried version.

INGREDIENTS

- 1 cup oil
- 4 cups water
- 1 teaspoon salt, plus more to taste
- 12 small broccoli florets
- ¾ cup all-purpose flour
- ¼ cup cornstarch
- ½ teaspoon baking powder
- 1 cup soda water
- Black pepper, to taste

1 Place the oil in a Dutch oven and heat to 350°F.

2 Place the water and salt in a medium saucepan and bring to a boil. Add the broccoli, cook for 3 minutes, remove and submerge in ice water. Remove and set on a paper towel to dry.

3 Combine ½ cup of the flour, the cornstarch, and the baking powder in a bowl. Pass through a sieve.

4 Add the soda water and whisk until smooth. This is the tempura mix.

5 In a small bowl, add the remaining flour and the broccoli. Mix gently until the broccoli is coated.

6 Dip the pieces of broccoli into the tempura mix. Drop in oil and fry until golden brown.

7 Use a slotted spoon to remove from the oil and set on a paper towel to drain. Season with salt and pepper and serve immediately.

Spring Salad with Green Goddess Dressing

YIELD: 4 SERVINGS • ACTIVE TIME: 20 MINUTES • TOTAL TIME: 40 MINUTES

The divine moniker is no accident—this dressing is thick and robust enough to lend body to this light salad, but delicate enough to keep you mindful of the fresh herbs that comprise it.

INGREDIENTS

For the Dressing

½ cup mayonnaise

⅔ cup buttermilk

1 tablespoon fresh lemon juice

2 tablespoons celery leaves, chopped

2 tablespoons fresh parsley leaves, chopped

2 tablespoons fresh tarragon, chopped

2 tablespoons fresh chives, sliced

2 teaspoons salt

1 teaspoon black pepper

For the Salad

Salt and pepper, to taste

6 asparagus stalks, trimmed and chopped

4 oz. snap peas, trimmed and chopped

3 heads of baby red leaf lettuce, halved

3 radishes, sliced thin with a mandoline, for garnish

Celery leaves, for garnish

1 Prepare the dressing. Place all of the ingredients in a food processor and puree until thoroughly combined. Transfer to a container and place in the refrigerator until ready to serve.

2 Bring a pot of salted water to a boil and prepare an ice water bath in a large bowl. Place the asparagus in the boiling water, cook for 1 minute, remove with a strainer, and transfer to bath until completely cool. Drain and transfer to a kitchen towel to dry.

3 Bring the water to a boil. Place the peas in the water, cook for 1 minute, remove with a strainer, and transfer to the water bath until completely cool. Transfer to a kitchen towel to dry.

4 Place the halved heads of lettuce on the serving plates. Place the asparagus and peas in a bowl, season with salt and pepper, and add the dressing. Toss to combine and place on top of the lettuce. Drizzle with additional dressing and garnish with the radishes and celery leaves.

Garden Sesame Noodles

YIELD: 6 SERVINGS • ACTIVE TIME: 15 MINUTES
TOTAL TIME: 30 MINUTES

Few Chinese dishes are as synonymous with take-out as sesame noodles, but the irony is that they are so easy to prepare and so much more delicious when homemade. This is the perfect dinner when you just want something light before curling up on the couch.

INGREDIENTS

1 pound rice stick noodles

2½ tablespoons toasted sesame oil

2 tablespoons tahini

1½ tablespoons smooth peanut butter

¼ cup soy sauce

2 tablespoons rice vinegar

1 tablespoon light brown sugar

2 teaspoons chili-garlic sauce, plus more to serve (optional)

2-inch piece of fresh ginger, peeled and grated

2 garlic cloves, minced

1 yellow or orange bell pepper, seeded and thinly sliced

1 cucumber, peeled, seeded, and thinly sliced

1 cup snow peas, trimmed

½ cup roasted peanuts, chopped, for garnish

2 tablespoons sesame seeds, toasted, for garnish

5 or 6 scallions, white and light green parts only, sliced into ½-inch pieces, for garnish

1 Bring a large pot of water to a boil. Add the noodles and cook until tender but still chewy, 2 to 3 minutes. Drain and transfer the noodles to a large bowl. Add ½ tablespoon of the sesame oil and toss to prevent them from sticking together.

2 Place the tahini and the peanut butter in a small bowl. Add the soy sauce, vinegar, remaining sesame oil, brown sugar, chili-garlic sauce (if using), ginger, and garlic and whisk together until smooth. Taste for seasoning and adjust the flavors according to your preference.

3 Add the sauce to the noodles and toss until well distributed. Arrange the noodles in six bowls and top with the pepper slivers, cucumber slices, and snow peas. Garnish with the peanuts, sesame seeds, and scallions and serve with additional chili-garlic sauce, if desired.

Pickled Ramps

YIELD: 2 SERVINGS • ACTIVE TIME: 5 MINUTES • TOTAL TIME: 2 HOURS

INGREDIENTS

½ cup champagne vinegar

½ cup water

¼ cup sugar

1½ teaspoons salt

¼ teaspoon fennel seeds

¼ teaspoon coriander seeds

⅛ teaspoon red pepper flakes

10 small ramp bulbs

1 Place all of the ingredients, except for the ramps, in a small saucepan and bring to a boil over medium heat.

2 Add the ramps, reduce the heat, and simmer for 1 minute. Transfer to a Mason jar, cover with plastic wrap, and let cool completely. Once cool, cover with a lid and store in the refrigerator for up to 1 week.

NOTE: TO DEBEARD THE MUSSELS, TAKE A FIRM GRIP ON THE HAIR THAT PROTRUDES FROM THE SHELL AND PULL UNTIL IT COMES FREE.

P.E.I. Mussels with Pickled Ramps

YIELD: 4 SERVINGS • ACTIVE TIME: 20 MINUTES • TOTAL TIME: 1 HOUR

The mussels from Prince Edward Island are naturally sweet and salty. Don't overlook the charred bread here, as it's a must for soaking up all of the leftover juices.

INGREDIENTS

1 lb. P.E.I. mussels

⅓ cup all-purpose flour

4 tablespoons unsalted butter

1 small shallot, chopped

2 garlic cloves, chopped

8 thin slices of fennel

½ cup cherry tomatoes

¼ cup white wine

¼ cup sliced Pickled Ramps (see sidebar)

Salt and pepper, to taste

4 slices of crusty bread

1 tablespoon olive oil

2 tablespoons fresh parsley leaves, chopped, for garnish

1 Place the mussels in a large bowl, cover with water, add the flour, and let soak for 30 minutes to ensure that the mussels aren't sandy. Drain the mussels and debeard them.

2 Place half of the butter in a large sauté pan and melt over high heat. Add the shallot, garlic, fennel, and tomatoes and cook, while continually shaking the pan, until the aromatics begin to brown and the tomatoes begin to blister. Add the mussels and deglaze the pan with the wine. Allow the alcohol to cook off, about 30 seconds, then add the remaining butter. Toss to coat the mussels and emulsify the sauce. Add the Pickled Ramps and a small pinch of salt and pepper. When the majority of the mussels have opened, remove from heat and set aside. Discard any mussels that did not open.

3 Turn on the broiler. Drizzle the bread with the olive oil and sprinkle with salt and pepper. Place beneath the broiler until it starts to char. Remove from the oven and set aside.

4 Ladle the mussels and sauce into warmed bowls, garnish with parsley, and serve with the charred bread.

Roasted Shrimp

YIELD: 10 TO 15 SERVINGS • ACTIVE TIME: 10 MINUTES
TOTAL TIME: 25 MINUTES

Tossing shrimp in the oven and crisping them slightly is a clever spin on the classic shrimp cocktail.

INGREDIENTS

2 lbs. fresh shrimp, shelled

3 tablespoons olive oil

2 teaspoons sea salt

2 teaspoons freshly ground black pepper

1 teaspoon red pepper flakes (optional)

1 Preheat oven to 400°F. Place all ingredients in a large bowl and toss until the shrimp are evenly coated.

2 Position the seasoned shrimp on a baking sheet in one layer. Bake for 9 to 10 minutes or until slightly browned. Serve warm or at room temperature.

Fall Salad and Cider Vinaigrette

YIELD: 4 TO 6 SERVINGS • ACTIVE TIME: 10 MINUTES • TOTAL TIME: 10 MINUTES

This lovely salad can handle the addition of almost any fruit, nut, or vegetable.

INGREDIENTS

For the Salad

1 head of butter lettuce, washed and spun dry

1 small head of radicchio, leaves pulled apart

1 handful of baby spinach

Flaky sea salt, to taste

For the Vinaigrette

4 tablespoons apple cider vinegar

1 tablespoon honey

3 tablespoons extra virgin olive oil

½ tablespoon kosher salt

¼ teaspoon black pepper

Flaky sea salt, to taste

1 Gently tear the lettuce leaves and radicchio leaves. Add them to a salad bowl with the baby spinach. Leave the baby spinach whole and place the greens in a large salad bowl.

2 To make the Cider Vinaigrette, combine the vinegar, honey, extra virgin olive oil, salt, and pepper in a bowl. Whisk to combine, sprinkle with sea salt, and set aside.

3 Spoon the vinaigrette over the salad greens. Toss gently until all salad greens are evenly dressed. Sprinkle with salt, toss, and serve.

Mike's Hot Honey Mustard Pork Skewers

YIELD: 8 SERVINGS • ACTIVE TIME: 20 MINUTES • TOTAL TIME: 1 HOUR

Looking to spice up your board a little bit? Give these skewers a try.

1 Place mustard, honey, and olive oil in a large bowl and stir until smooth. Add pork cubes and toss to coat. Set aside.

2 Soak 8 bamboo skewers in cold water for 20 minutes. Preheat broiler to high and line a broiling pan with foil.

3 Divide pork and peppers into 8 portions and alternate them on the skewers. Season with salt and pepper.

4 Broil or grill for 10 to 15 minutes, turning often until slightly browned and cooked through.

INGREDIENTS

¼ cup Dijon mustard

¼ cup Mike's Hot Honey

1 tablespoon olive oil

1 ½ lbs. pork tenderloin, cut into 1-inch cubes

8 bamboo skewers

2 bell peppers, seeded and chopped

Salt and pepper, to taste

Zucchini Fritters with Sumac Yogurt

YIELD: 4 SERVINGS • ACTIVE TIME: 15 MINUTES • TOTAL TIME: 30 MINUTES

Zucchini has a number of wonderful uses, and turning it into fritters is one of the easiest ways to get people excited about this summer squash. Staghorn sumac is massively underutilized (outside of Middle Eastern cuisine). By using it as an accent here, you can remedy that oversight.

INGREDIENTS

1½ lbs. zucchini, grated

Salt and pepper, to taste

¼ cup all-purpose flour

¼ cup Parmesan cheese, grated

1 egg, beaten

3 tablespoons canola oil

1 cup yogurt

2 teaspoons fresh lemon juice

2 tablespoons sumac powder

1 Line a colander with cheesecloth and then place the zucchini in the colander, salt them, and let stand for 1 hour. Then press down to remove as much water from the zucchini as you can.

2 Place the zucchini, flour, Parmesan, and egg in a mixing bowl and stir to combine.

3 Use your hands to form handfuls of the mixture into balls and then gently press down on the balls to form them into patties.

4 Place the canola oil in a cast-iron skillet and warm over medium-high heat.

5 Working in batches, place the patties into the oil, taking care not to crowd the skillet. Cook until golden brown, about 5 minutes. Flip them over and cook for another 5 minutes, until the fritters are also golden brown on that side. Remove from the skillet and drain on a paper towel–lined plate.

6 Place the yogurt, lemon juice, and sumac powder in a small bowl and stir to combine.

7 Season the fritters with salt and pepper and serve the yogurt on the side.

Dill Pickle Arancini

YIELD: 8 TO 10 SERVINGS • ACTIVE TIME: 30 MINUTES • TOTAL TIME: 45 MINUTES

It's not easy to outshine a fried, golden coating, but the multifaceted flavor of dill somehow manages to do just that in this dish.

INGREDIENTS

For the Cajun Remoulade:

1 cup mayonnaise

2 tablespoons Dijon mustard

1 teaspoon hot sauce

2 teaspoons Cajun seasoning

Zest and juice of 1 lemon

1 garlic clove, minced

For the Arancini:

8 cups chicken stock

1 stick unsalted butter

2 cups Arborio rice

1 small white onion, minced

1 cup white wine

1½ cups Havarti cheese with dill, grated

1½ cups dill pickles of choice, chopped

Salt and pepper, to taste

4 cups canola or vegetable oil

6 large eggs, beaten

5 cups panko bread crumbs

1 To make Cajun Remoulade, combine all ingredients in a medium bowl, then refrigerate until ready to serve.

2 To make the Arancini, heat the chicken stock in a pot until simmering. In a separate pot, melt the butter over high heat.

3 Once the butter is bubbling, add the rice and the onion and cook until the onion becomes translucent, about 4 minutes.

4 Deglaze the pot with the white wine and reduce until the wine has almost completely evaporated. Then, reduce the heat to medium-high and begin adding the hot chicken stock ¼ cup at a time, stirring frequently until incorporated and reduced slightly. Continue this process until all the liquid has been added and the rice is cooked.

5 Turn off the heat and add the cheese and pickles, seasoning with salt and pepper to taste. Pour the mixture onto a sheet tray and let cool.

6 Meanwhile, place the oil in a large pot and cook over medium heat until it reaches 350°F.

7 Once the risotto mixture is cool, form into golf ball-sized spheres. Submerge in the eggs, then coat with the bread crumbs.

8 Place the balls in the oil and cook until warmed through and golden brown on the outside.

9 Serve with Cajun Remoulade.

Blue Cheese Fritters

YIELD: 4 TO 6 SERVINGS • ACTIVE TIME: 15 MINUTES • TOTAL TIME: 30 MINUTES

Using Cashel Blue adds a touch of class to what is traditionally thought of as pub food.

INGREDIENTS

2 cups oil

3 eggs, beaten

¼ cup all-purpose flour

1 cup panko bread crumbs, reduced to a fine powder in a food processor

6 oz. Cashel Blue cheese, rolled into 12 balls or cut into 12 cubes

Salt, to taste

1 Place the oil in a medium saucepan and heat to 350°F.

2 Place the eggs in a bowl. Place the flour and bread crumbs in separate bowls.

3 Dredge the balls of cheese in the flour, remove, and shake to remove excess flour. Place the floured cheese in the egg wash and coat evenly. Remove from egg wash, shake to remove excess egg, and gently coat with bread crumbs.

4 Place the balls in the hot oil and fry until golden brown. Use a slotted spoon to remove from the oil. Set on paper towels to drain and season with salt. Allow to cool slightly before serving.

Corn Beignets

The corn kernels add a wonderful texture to these pillowy, fried balls of dough.

1 In a medium saucepan, add milk, salt, and butter. Bring to a boil.

2 Add the flour and stir constantly until a ball of dough forms.

3 Remove the pan from heat. Let the dough cool for 10 minutes.

4 Add the egg to the pan and whisk vigorously.

5 Once the egg is combined, add the corn and cilantro. Stir until combined.

6 Place the oil in a Dutch oven and heat to 350°F.

7 Spoon small amounts of batter into the hot oil and cook until golden brown.

8 Remove with a slotted spoon and set on a paper towel to drain. Serve when cool enough to handle.

INGREDIENTS

¼ cup milk

⅛ teaspoon salt

2 tablespoons unsalted butter

¼ cup flour

1 egg

¼ cup corn kernels

½ teaspoon fresh cilantro, chopped

2 cups oil

Artisanal Cheese Ball

This cheese ball recipe is a stand-alone hit on any board and a great textural diversion on a larger spread. To make it vegetarian, substitute smoked almonds for the bacon.

INGREDIENTS

6 oz. fromage blanc

3 oz. aged cheddar cheese, finely grated

3 oz. blue cheese, crumbled

½ tablespoon sour cream

1 or 2 dashes Worcestershire sauce

¼ teaspoon garlic powder

¼ teaspoon fresh cracked black pepper

⅛ teaspoon salt

2 green onions, thinly sliced

1 cup bacon, minced

Assorted crackers, to serve

1 Combine the cheeses, sour cream, Worcestershire sauce, garlic powder, pepper, and salt in a food processor or the bowl of a standing mixer. Puree or beat on low for 3 minutes or until mixture is smooth.

2 Fold in the green onions, place mixture in a large bowl, and shape into a ball with a large mixing spoon. Chill for at least 1 hour.

3 Meanwhile, cook bacon in a skillet over medium heat for about 6 minutes until crisp. Drain on paper towels.

4 Dice or crumble and set aside.

5 Gently remove cheese ball from bowl and spread bacon bits on wax paper or cutting board. Roll the cheese ball until evenly coated.

6 Serve at room temperature with assorted crackers.

Gribiche

Don't be put off by the name: this dish is easy to make and can be thrown together in a hurry.

1 Separate the egg whites and yolks of the hardboiled eggs. Place the yolks into a bowl. Chop the whites and reserve.

2 Add the mustard, lemon juice, capers, salt, and pepper into the bowl containing the yolks.

3 Using a whisk, mash the yolks until completely disbursed. Then, slowly whisk in the olive oil.

4 Once mixed, add the egg whites and the herbs. Stir until fully incorporated and serve.

INGREDIENTS

11 eggs, hardboiled

6 tablespoons mustard

6 tablespoons lemon juice

4 tablespoons capers, chopped

2 teaspoons salt

2 tablespoons white pepper

1 cup olive oil

2 teaspoons fresh parsley, chiffonade

½ teaspoon fresh tarragon, minced

½ teaspoon fresh chervil, minced

3 tablespoons fresh chives, minced

Desserts

If your sweet tooth is craving some attention after so much savory goodness, the recipes in this chapter not only make for excellent after-dinner treats, they also lend themselves to being presented on serving boards. And remember, if you use cast iron, once the pan has cooled down, you can just set it on the table and let everyone help themselves.

Honey Roasted Figs

YIELD: 4 SERVINGS • ACTIVE TIME: 5 MINUTES • TOTAL TIME: 10 MINUTES

The honey and cinnamon accentuate the sweetness and nuttiness that figs are famous for, while the goat cheese adds a luxurious creaminess.

INGREDIENTS

2 tablespoons honey

4 black mission figs, halved

⅛ teaspoon cinnamon

Goat cheese, crumbled, to taste

1 In a medium nonstick sauté pan, add the honey and warm over medium heat.

2 Place the cut figs facedown and cook for 5 minutes, or until golden brown.

3 Sprinkle the cinnamon over the figs and gently stir to coat. Remove figs from the pan and serve with crumbled goat cheese.

Creamy Lemon Curd

This is the perfect palate cleanser after hours of snacking on rich meats and cheeses.

1 In a medium mixing bowl, mix together the egg yolks, sugar, salt, and lemon juice.

2 Place mixture in medium saucepan over low heat.

3 Using a rubber spatula, stir continuously until the mixture begins to thicken. Make sure to maintain a low temperature. Do not boil.

4 Once thickened, remove the pot from the heat and pour the curd through a strainer into a bowl.

5 Add the lemon zest, whisk in the cubed butter until combined, then add the cream cheese and whisk until smooth.

INGREDIENTS

12 large egg yolks

1½ cups sugar

Pinch of salt

1 cup lemon juice

6 tablespoons lemon zest

½ lb. unsalted butter, cut into cubes

12 oz. cream cheese, at room temperature

Tiramisu Dip

YIELD: 2 TO 3 CUPS • ACTIVE TIME: 10 MINUTES • TOTAL TIME: 30 MINUTES

Serve this dip with ladyfingers and your fruit of choice for an instant favorite.

INGREDIENTS

1⅓ cups mascarpone cheese

½ cup ricotta cheese

½ cup powdered sugar

1 teaspoon pure vanilla extract

2 tablespoons brewed espresso

1 teaspoon fine espresso powder

2 tablespoons Kahlua

1 teaspoon cocoa powder

½ cup semi-sweet chocolate chips, chopped

Ladyfingers and fruit of choice, to serve

1 In a standing mixer, beat together the cheeses, sugar, vanilla, brewed espresso, espresso powder, and Kahlua until thoroughly combined.

2 Place in a serving dish, dust with cocoa powder, and sprinkle with the chocolate chips. Place in refrigerator until chilled. Serve with ladyfingers and fruit of choice.

Brownie Batter Dip

YIELD: 1½ CUPS • ACTIVE TIME: 5 MINUTES • TOTAL TIME: 5 MINUTES

A perfect complement to the tangy sweetness of strawberries, this dip is chocolate heaven.

1 If using cream cheese, soften it and the butter in microwave for 20 to 30 seconds each, stirring every 5 seconds to achieve the desired consistency.

2 Beat softened cream cheese or yogurt and butter in a bowl until thoroughly combined.

3 Add remaining ingredients and mix until smooth. Serve with fresh strawberries and shortbread.

INGREDIENTS

8 oz. cream cheese or plain Greek yogurt

1 stick unsalted butter

1½ cups powdered sugar

½ cup cocoa powder

2 tablespoons brown sugar

⅓ cup whole milk

1 teaspoon vanilla extract

½ teaspoon sea salt

Fresh strawberries and shortbread, to serve

Chocolate Hazelnut Dip

YIELD: 1 TO 1½ CUPS • ACTIVE TIME: 15 TO 20 MINUTES
TOTAL TIME: 30 TO 40 MINUTES

A homemade version of Nutella®, the dip that stole our hearts, this beloved spread brings a hint of umami to any desert board.

INGREDIENTS

2 cups hazelnuts

⅓ cup sugar

1 teaspoon sea salt

16 oz. semi-sweet chocolate, chopped

1 stick unsalted butter

1 cup heavy whipping cream

1 Preheat the oven to 350°F. Remove the outer shell from the hazelnuts using a nutcracker.

2 Layer the shelled hazelnuts on a baking sheet in one even layer. Roast in oven for 12 to 15 minutes, then remove and let cool.

3 Place cooled hazelnuts, sugar, and salt into a food processor and blend until the mixture forms a paste.

4 Meanwhile, boil ½-inch of water in a saucepan. Set a bowl over the boiling water, making sure the water does not touch the bowl. This is your double boiler. Add the chocolate to the bowl and allow to melt.

5 Once melted, remove from heat and whisk in the butter and cream. Then, combine the chocolate mixture and the hazelnut paste.

6 Chill before serving.

Cinnamon Twists

YIELD: 12 TO 15 SERVINGS • ACTIVE TIME: 15 TO 20 MINUTES
TOTAL TIME: 30 MINUTES

These twists are good enough to serve as the centerpiece of your board. Pair with the Chocolate Hazelnut Dip (see page 258) and you have a combination fit for royalty.

1 Preheat oven to 375°F. Roll out puff pastry sheets until each is 10 by 12 inches.

2 Combine sugar, cinnamon, and nutmeg in a bowl.

3 Lightly brush the tops of each pastry sheet with the egg. Then, sprinkle the sugar-and-spice mixture evenly across the tops of both sheets.

4 Cut the pastries into long strips and twist. Place strips on a baking sheet and bake for 12 to 15 minutes, or until golden brown. Flip each pastry and allow to cook for an additional 2 to 3 minutes.

5 Remove twists from oven and allow to cool until slightly warm. Serve with your favorite dip.

INGREDIENTS

2 sheets of puff pastry, thawed

1 cup sugar

3½ tablespoons cinnamon

1 teaspoon freshly ground nutmeg

1 egg, beaten

Citrus-Rosemary Shortbread

Serve these simple citrus cookies, flecked with rosemary, on a wooden board with a pot of tea.

1 Preheat oven to 350°F and line a baking sheet with parchment paper.

2 Place all of the ingredients in a mixing bowl, except the flour and demerara sugar, and beat at low speed until creamy.

3 Slowly add the flour until the dough is the consistency of coarse crumbs.

4 Press dough into a long cube and chill for 1 hour.

5 Slice the dough into squares or form into rounds. Then, place on the baking sheet, and sprinkle with demerara sugar.

6 Bake for 15 minutes, or until lightly golden brown.

7 Remove from the oven, let cool, and serve. If working with square shortbread, slice into wedges before serving.

INGREDIENTS

2 cups unsalted butter, softened

¼ cup sugar

¼ cup lemon or orange juice

3 teaspoons lemon or orange zest

2 teaspoons fresh rosemary, minced

4½ cups all-purpose flour

Demerara sugar, to taste

Chocolate Fondue

YIELD: 4 SERVINGS • ACTIVE TIME: 5 MINUTES • TOTAL TIME: 10 MINUTES

This classic chocolate fondue goes perfectly with whatever seasonal fruit is available. It pairs particularly well with white peaches.

INGREDIENTS

12 oz. bittersweet chocolate, chopped

¾ cup heavy cream

1 teaspoon vanilla extract

1 Combine ingredients in a glass bowl.

2 Place the bowl in the microwave and microwave for 2 minutes, or until melted.

3 Stir until smooth and serve immediately.

4 If you want the sauce to remain warm, it can be placed in a traditional fondue pot with a lit burner.

Chocolate-Dipped Strawberries

Question: Who can resist strawberries dipped in chocolate?
Answer: No one!

1 Line a baking sheet with parchment or wax paper.

2 Pour chocolate chips into a glass bowl and melt in microwave by cooking for about 1 to 2 minutes or until chips are melted completely.

3 While chocolate is hot, dip each strawberry halfway into the melted chocolate.

4 Place on lined baking sheet.

5 When all the strawberries have been dipped, place baking sheet in the refrigerator and chill until the chocolate is set.

INGREDIENTS

12 oz. white, milk, or dark chocolate chips

1 pint fresh strawberries, preferably with long stems

Gluten-Free Macaroon Bites

YIELD: 8 SERVINGS • ACTIVE TIME: 15 MINUTE • TOTAL TIME: 1 HOUR

These delicious bites are sure to be an after-dinner favorite.

INGREDIENTS

1¼ cups sugar

4 cups unsweetened coconut flakes

4 egg whites

2 teaspoons vanilla extract

¼ teaspoon salt

1 Preheat oven to 350°F. While preheating, place a cast-iron skillet in the oven to warm up.

2 In a large bowl, combine all ingredients.

3 Once the oven has finished heating, remove the skillet. Pour the batter into the pan or roll into balls and dollop into skillet and place back into the oven.

4 Bake for 20 to 30 minutes or until brown on top.

5 Remove the skillet and allow to cool for about 30 minutes. If baking in a round, slice into wedges before serving.

Classic Shortbread Cookies

YIELD: 6 TO 8 SERVINGS • ACTIVE TIME: 25 MINUTES • TOTAL TIME: 1½ HOURS

Perfect for hot summer days with fresh strawberries or cold fall evenings with a cup of coffee, these shortbread cookies are good to go all year long.

INGREDIENTS

1 cup flour, plus more for dusting

¼ teaspoon salt

¼ cup sugar

1 stick unsalted butter, chilled

½ teaspoon vanilla extract

1 Preheat oven to 300°F. Place a cast-iron skillet in the oven to warm while making the dough.

2 In a large bowl, whisk the flour, salt, and sugar until combined.

3 Cut the chilled butter into slices and add to the flour mixture. Work with your hands until the mixture starts to come together, then add the vanilla extract. Continue to work the mixture until it resembles a coarse meal.

4 Form the dough into a ball, then place on a lightly floured surface and roll out into circles. The circle should be slightly smaller than the diameter of your skillet, about 8 inches. Slice into 8 wedges. Or, if desired, shape into circles with a cookie cutter and place in skillet ½-inch apart.

5 Remove the skillet from the oven and place the circles into the pan. Place the skillet back into the oven and bake for 45 minutes or until shortbread is a pale golden color.

6 Remove the skillet and allow to cool for 10 minutes, then serve.

French Apple Tart

YIELD: 6 TO 8 SERVINGS • ACTIVE TIME: 1 HOUR • TOTAL TIME: 2 TO 24 HOURS

This is a gorgeous dessert that is sure to wow your guests.

INGREDIENTS

1 cup flour

½ teaspoon salt

1 cup sugar, plus 1 tablespoon

9 tablespoons unsalted butter, cut into small pieces

3 tablespoons ice water

1 teaspoon cinnamon

8 to 10 apples, peeled, cored, and sliced

1 To make the pastry, whisk together the flour, salt, and 1 tablespoon of sugar in a large bowl. Using your fingers, work 6 tablespoons of the butter into the flour mixture until you have coarse clumps. Sprinkle the ice water over the mixture and continue to work it with your hands until the dough just holds together. Shape it into a ball, wrap it in plastic wrap, and refrigerate it for at least 1 hour or overnight.

2 Preparation for the tart starts in a cast-iron skillet. Place the remaining pieces of butter evenly over the bottom of the skillet, then sprinkle the remaining sugar and the cinnamon evenly over everything. Cook over medium heat until the mixture is melted together and starts to brown slightly. Next, place the apple slices in the pan. The slices should overlap and face the same direction. Place either 1 or 2 slices in the center when finished working around the outside. As the tart bakes, the slices will slide down a bit.

3 Place the skillet on the stove and turn the heat to medium-high. Cook the apples in the pan, uncovered, until the sugar and butter start to caramelize, about 10 to 15 minutes. While they're cooking, spoon some of the melted juices over the apples (but don't overdo it).

4 Preheat the oven to 400°F and position a rack in the center.

5 Take the chilled dough out of the refrigerator and, working on a lightly floured surface, roll it out into a circle just big enough to cover the skillet (about 12 to 14 inches). Gently drape the pastry over the apples, tucking it in around the sides. Put the skillet in the oven and bake for about 25 minutes, until the pastry is golden brown. Remove the skillet from the oven and allow to cool for about 5 minutes.

6 Find a plate that is an inch or 2 larger than the top of the skillet and place it over the top. You will be inverting the tart onto the plate. Be sure to use oven mitts or secure pot holders, as the skillet will be hot.

7 Holding the plate tightly against the top of the skillet, turn the skillet over so the plate is now on the bottom. If some of the apples are stuck to the bottom, gently remove them and place them on the tart. Allow to cool for a few more minutes, then serve.

Pumpkin Pecan Tart

YIELD: 6 TO 8 SERVINGS • ACTIVE TIME: 1 HOUR • TOTAL TIME: 1½ HOURS

In a twist on a traditional pumpkin pie, this tart has the pecans as the crust for a delicious result.

INGREDIENTS

1½ cups raw pecans

1½ tablespoons honey

2 tablespoons unsalted butter, chilled and cut into small pieces, plus 1 tablespoon for greasing the skillet

1 (15 oz.) can pumpkin puree

1 (12 oz.) can evaporated milk

2 eggs, lightly beaten

¾ cup granulated sugar

1 teaspoon ground cinnamon

¼ teaspoon ground ginger

¼ teaspoon ground allspice

½ teaspoon salt

1 cup heavy cream

2 tablespoons confectioners' sugar

Pumpkin seeds, for garnish

1 Preheat the oven to 400°F.

2 Put the pecans in a food processor and pulse until you have a coarse, crumbly meal. Alternately, you can put the pecans in a large, thick plastic bag and mash them with a rolling pin or meat tenderizer.

3 Transfer the crushed nuts to a bowl and add the honey and butter, mixing with a pastry blender, fork, or your fingers until a coarse meal is formed. There can be chunks of butter.

4 Liberally grease a cast-iron skillet with the butter. Transfer the nut mixture to the skillet and gently press it into the pan to form a crust.

5 Put the skillet on top of a cookie sheet to catch any oil that may spatter. Bake for 10 to 12 minutes, until browned and toasted. Remove from the oven and allow to cool completely on a wire rack.

6 Reduce the oven's temperature to 350°F.

7 In a large bowl, stir together the pumpkin puree and evaporated milk. Add the eggs and stir to combine. Add the sugar, cinnamon, ginger, allspice, and salt and stir to combine thoroughly.

8 Working with the crust in the skillet, transfer the pumpkin mixture into the crust.

9 Put the skillet in the oven and bake for about 50 minutes, until a knife inserted near the center comes out clean. Remove the skillet from the oven and allow to cool completely.

10 Before serving, beat the heavy cream with an electric mixer until soft peaks form. Add the confectioners' sugar 1 tablespoon at a time until it has dissolved and stiff peaks form. Serve the tart with whipped cream and garnish with pumpkin seeds.

Peach Galette

When peaches are ripe in the mid-to-late summer, this is a super-simple way to turn them into a great dessert.

INGREDIENTS

2½ cups flour, plus more for dusting

1 teaspoon salt

¼ cup vegetable shortening

½ cup salted butter, chilled and cut into small pieces (if using unsalted butter, increase salt to 1¼ teaspoons), plus 1 tablespoon for greasing the skillet

6 to 8 tablespoons cold water

3 cups fresh peaches, peeled, pitted, and sliced

½ cup sugar, plus 1 tablespoon

Juice of ½ lemon

3 tablespoons cornstarch

Pinch of salt

2 tablespoons peach jam

1 teaspoon Amaretto liqueur (optional)

1 egg, beaten

Raspberries, for garnish (optional)

1 In a large bowl, combine the flour and salt. Add the shortening and, using a fork, work it in until the mixture forms a very coarse meal. Add the butter and work into the dough with a pastry blender or your fingers until the dough is just holding together. Don't overwork the dough.

2 Add 4 tablespoons cold water to start and, using your hands or a fork, work the dough, adding additional tablespoons of water until the dough just holds together when you gather it in your hands.

3 Working on a lightly floured surface, gather the dough and form it into a solid ball. Wrap tightly in plastic wrap and refrigerate for 30 to 60 minutes.

4 Take the dough out of the refrigerator to allow it to warm up slightly. While still cold, place the refrigerated dough on a lightly floured surface and flatten with a floured rolling pin, working both sides to extend each into a 9- to 12-inch round.

5 Grease a cast-iron skillet with 1 tablespoon of butter. Carefully position the crust in the skillet so it is evenly distributed, pressing it in lightly and allowing the dough to extend over the side. The crust in the skillet should be slightly larger than the bottom of the pan so that it can be folded over.

6 Preheat oven to 400°F. In a large bowl, mix the peaches with ½ cup of sugar, lemon juice, cornstarch, and salt. Stir well to be sure to coat all the fruit.

7 If using the liqueur, mix it with the jam in a small bowl before smearing the jam on the center of the crust.

8 Place the fruit in a mound in the center of the crust. Fold the edge of the crust over to cover about 1 inch of filling. Brush the crust with the beaten egg and sprinkle with the remaining sugar.

9 Put the skillet in the oven and bake until the filling is bubbly, which is necessary for it to thicken sufficiently, about 35 to 40 minutes.

10 Remove the skillet from the oven and allow to cool. If using, garnish with raspberries before serving.

Metric Equivalents

Weights

1 ounce	28 grams
2 ounces	57 grams
4 ounces (¼ pound)	113 grams
8 ounces (½ pound)	227 grams
16 ounces (1 pound)	454 grams

Volume Measures

⅛ teaspoon		0.6 ml
¼ teaspoon		1.23 ml
½ teaspoon		2.5 ml
1 teaspoon		5 ml
1 tablespoon (3 teaspoons)	½ fluid ounce	15 ml
2 tablespoons	1 fluid ounce	29.5 ml
¼ cup (4 tablespoons)	2 fluid ounces	59 ml
⅓ cup (5⅓ tablespoons)	2.7 fluid ounces	80 ml
½ cup (8 tablespoons)	4 fluid ounces	120 ml
⅔ cup (10⅔ tablespoons)	5.4 fluid ounces	160 ml
¾ cup (12 tablespoons)	6 fluid ounces	180 ml
1 cup (16 tablespoons)	8 fluid ounces	240 ml

Temperature Equivalents

°F	°C	Gas Mark
225	110	¼
250	130	½
275	140	1
300	150	2
325	170	3
350	180	4
375	190	5
400	200	6
425	220	7
450	230	8
475	240	9
500	250	10

Length Measures

¹⁄₁₆-inch	1.6 mm
⅛-inch	3 mm
¼-inch	1.35 mm
½-inch	1.25 cm
¾-inch	2 cm
1-inch	2.5 cm

Index

ABOUT CIDER MILL PRESS BOOK PUBLISHERS

Good ideas ripen with time. From seed to harvest, Cider Mill
Press brings fine reading, information, and entertainment
together between the covers of its creatively crafted books.
Our Cider Mill bears fruit twice a year, publishing
a new crop of titles each spring and fall.

"Where Good Books Are Ready for Press"

VISIT US ONLINE:
cidermillpress.com

OR WRITE TO US AT
PO Box 454
12 Spring St.
Kennebunkport, Maine 04046